Manouche

Manouche

*Living with the
Gypsies of France*

NIGEL PARSONS

THE CHOIR PRESS

First published in the United Kingdom in 2019 by
The Choir Press

ISBN 978-1-78963-065-7

I dedicate this book to both of my 'families': to my own real one, whose names are all mentioned in the story and to whom I am deeply grateful for putting up with me while it was written, not to mention beforehand and afterwards, in fact all of the time, and to my Manouche one who adopted me and so made this tale possible.

Contents

CONTENTS

First Encounters

———

The first of the adults to speak to me was, surprisingly, a woman. Tiny, birdlike Ghuno, of indeterminate age, with dyed yellow hair tied back in a bun above jet-black eyebrows, barefoot and wearing mismatched clothes that could have come from any jumble sale. And probably did.

'My name is Ghuno,' she said, standing several feet away and looking down, 'and I wanted to thank you for the sweets you've been giving the children.'

'You're welcome.' I half-smiled, a bit embarrassed. I was fascinated but unsure of these people who all the French said to stay away from. They didn't really look the way I imagined Gypsies should. There were no horse-drawn *vardas*, caravans, or violin sessions around the campfire. The women weren't wearing long flowered skirts or coloured head-scarves, while the men were scruffy and argumentative. They looked more like a ragtag group of refugees, and I wondered if they weren't real Gypsies at all, but just drop-outs looking for an easy life on the dole. 'Who are you people? Where do you come from?'

Ghuno took a step closer and looked up, her sparkling nut-brown eyes both defiant and wary. 'We are Manouche, who some call the Sinti, and we are from everywhere and nowhere. Maybe some of us lived in Germany once, and some in Spain. Other than that I do not know; we are free people. And you?'

'I'm from England, it's ...'

'I've heard of it,' she said, and walked away.

In time we were to become close friends. I learned she was in her early thirties, but she looked much older, with her skin burned dark by the sun and heavily lined, and she never let me forget that it was she who spoke to me before any of the others.

1

We were in the Gironde, about twenty-five miles east of Bordeaux, and for two weeks we'd been working on the *vendange*, the grape harvest. It was hard work but fulfilling; being outdoors all day and going to sleep tired at night is one of the best feelings in the world. Using secateurs to cut the grapes and hauling them in huge buckets to the tractor trailer was backbreaking, but the food was good and everyone got a litre of wine a day.

I'd gone after meeting Jean-Pierre, the son of the patron, Pierre Renaudat, in London. Jean-Pierre and I had become good friends, and he'd invited me over for the *vendange* at their minor chateau, Tête Rouge, in the village of Saint-André-de-Cubzac, not far from the market town of Libourne. His father was a tall and elegant man who was a senior manager with an oil company, and he welcomed me into their house, where we enjoyed many a long evening over delicious meals conjured up by his wife Suzanne, drinking his wine and chewing over the cud of politics. He'd never been to England but had a keen interest in the country which he said Europe needed as a counterbalance to Germany, even if England at that time was racked by strikes and was known widely as the sick man of Europe.

Apart from the five Manouche families, there were half a dozen French students, and me. While we worked under the warm September sun, the Manouche children ran all day amongst the vines on a non-stop energy supply. They were a bewildering mixture of hues, a few very blond, others black-haired but with transparently blue eyes that contrasted strikingly with their dark skin, and still others light brown with wide almond eyes, who reminded me of native or mixed children from South America. Some were naked or half-dressed, and all were filthy from early morning until their evening wash. They didn't share either, at least not outside their immediate brothers or sisters; if I gave one ten sweets, then he or she would be gone. So after the first time the sweets had to be allocated individually. This was a trait that carried on to a greater or lesser degree into adulthood.

As the harvest drew to a close, everyone began to focus on the feast that the patron was sure to put on, the Manouche children conjuring up images of the cakes and fizzy drinks that would be their special treat. It was held in a barn, alongside and in full view of the Manouche camp, but there wasn't a single Gypsy inside. They hadn't been invited; in fact, they'd been told they weren't welcome. This was to be a 'whites only' affair.

We sipped our aperitifs and sat down to a typically formal and sumptuous French dinner with multiple courses. A couple of the French students seemed faintly embarrassed about the exclusion of the Manouche, while I busied myself getting angrily drunk.

It was late already when we heard a guitar playing outside the door and the sound of children singing. I opened the door and a young boy was sitting on the top stair, strumming and tapping his guitar in the Spanish way, while below him half a dozen others had formed a circle around a beautiful dark-haired girl dancing a flamenco. She was Ghuno's daughter Bianca, who I would later come to know well. Georges, the portly and ruddy-faced peasant who was the head *vendangeur*, waved his arms and told them to be off. In the ensuing confusion I scooped up several cakes from the dessert table and thrust them into the arms of the Manouche children as they were hustled away.

The party, if that's what it was, wound down quickly after that, and I stumbled over to the Manouche camp. The fires were low and no one was outside, and I tripped and fell full-length into a muddied puddle between two caravans, lying there until one of the French students kindly came to fetch me.

The next morning, when I tried again to visit the camp, all I found were the muddy tyre tracks of the caravans and cars and the blackened, burnt-out remnants of the fires. The Manouche were gone.

*

Back in London I thought that my brief Gypsy experience was over, but I couldn't shake off thoughts of the Manouche; it was like a spell. I loved their free spirit, the music, the campfires and the closeness.

In a way, that wasn't surprising. I'd travelled all my life to all corners of the world, going wherever the army sent my father – Egypt, Singapore, Malaya (as it was then), Nepal and Germany – until I left school and just carried on drifting. After an apprenticeship with the *Cambridge Evening News* I told the editor I was giving up journalism and went to travel again, through Italy, Greece and Turkey, Iran and Afghanistan. In Afghanistan I rode a horse along with a German traveller and his Swiss girlfriend for several weeks, past the ancient and famous Bamiyan statues of Buddha, since destroyed by the Taliban, up to the crystal turquoise lakes of Band-e Amir. It was freezing cold outside, but the simple huts where we slept with the villagers had an ingenious system of heated water pipes running under the mud floors, the first under-floor heating I'd come across, and we were snug.

I crossed the Khyber Pass into Pakistan, took a train down into India, flew from Calcutta to Thailand, and travelled by train to Malaysia and on to Singapore, where I used most of my depleted funds to board a ship to Australia, eventually washing up almost penniless in Perth. There I signed up for six months to work in an iron ore mine in the middle of nowhere, in the arid northwest of the country.

We worked for seven days a week sometimes, up to sixteen hours a day, but there was nothing else to do. After six months I had more money than I'd ever imagined before and started moving again, to New Zealand first, where I briefly returned to work as a reporter on the *New Zealand Herald*, then up through southeast Asia to Hong Kong, this time finding work with the local state radio station.

That came to a sudden end when I heard that my mother was seriously ill and I rushed back to England to help look after her. My sister Diane also came back from the United States to help. To this day we don't really know what was wrong with her, but it was probably dementia or Alzheimer's, which were poorly understood at the time. In any event the doctors prescribed ever-increasing doses of Valium as treatment, which probably only accelerated her condition, until she hardly knew where she was or recognised any of us, and it was almost a relief when she caught pneumonia and passed away in January of 1976. After the funeral at the village church in Arborfield in Berkshire, Diane went back to America, but I felt unable to leave my father alone straight away.

It was during the winter of the following year, while I continued to work as a freelancer wherever I could while paying regular visits to the family home, that I first met Jean-Pierre in London, where he was on holiday. We instantly forged a friendship which lasts to this day, and he invited me to come to Bordeaux for my first *vendange* the year after, in 1978.

The constant moving meant I didn't feel I really belonged anywhere, and with the Manouche I felt that bond of the road. In the end I think all nomads, whatever level their nomadic life is lived on, belong to the same netherworld; we're all running from nowhere to nowhere. We might try to dress it up as freedom, but the reality is people keep moving because they have no roots, no land to call their own, just the fugitive mentality of outsiders. Maybe it goes some way to explaining how and why I identified with the Manouche, and maybe it goes some way also to explaining why they one day accepted me as one of their own. But the first question was how to find them again.

A Strike

The answer was obvious, but it meant waiting a year. I called Jean-Pierre and asked if I could come back to Tête Rouge for the following harvest and bring some friends as well. He readily agreed and promised a warm welcome, and at the end of summer I put together a small group and drove them in my trusty blue Bedford van to Tête Rouge, more in hope than expectation.

There were five of us. Apart from myself there was Ernesto Ferreira (a Brazilian doctor who I'm still in touch with), Margeurita Serje (a friend from Colombia who the last I heard was on an archaeological dig in the Lost City, Colombia's answer to Machu Picchu on the Sierra Nevada de Santa Marta, overlooking the Caribbean sea), and two others from England, Andy McConnell (who would later become one of the UK's leading experts on antique glass and a regular guest on the BBC's *Antiques Roadshow*) and Liz Strawson (who resurfaced recently on social media and now lives in Ely, north of Cambridge). We arrived well in advance of the *vendange* and booked our places, but there was no sign of the Manouche.

While we waited we went to the Basque country in northwestern Spain, hanging out on the beach in San Sebastián, busking for money in the evenings until the Guardia Civil moved us on. It's a beautiful city, built around a wide golden bay, with narrow cobbled streets in the old town full of tapas bars and fresh fish restaurants. But the Basque country was still a tense place in 1979; Franco was not long gone and the Basque separatists from ETA were active.

When the harvest was imminent, we drove back to the Gironde, and as we approached the small village of Saint-André-de-Cubzac again we spotted the ubiquitous blue Renault and Saviem vans and caravans of the Manouche. I realised they were the same ones and my heart missed a beat; we'd found them and I was ecstatic. But I'd never have expected the excited welcome they gave us – or at least the children did.

A stream of them came running down the path towards us, Bianca, Lele, Mooka, La Muette and others, shouting, '*Nadjo, Nadjo, arjha tu?*': 'how are you?' Thrusting their sticky hands into mine, they led us to the campsite, and there were Ghuno and the men: Chocote, Meme, Paquili, Mochi and young Roupenho. They all waved and smiled a welcome and brought out wine, a few drops for Mother Earth first and a cup for each of us. There were no handshakes or hugs, but it was like meeting old friends again, and during the ensuing weeks that's exactly what we became.

Meme was the first man, or *rom*, to befriend me in their *kumpania*, or company, of five families. The younger brother by a couple of years of Chocote, the company's head, Meme was a mountain of a man in his early forties, with a sparse moustache, tall for a Manouche and with a stomach that extended so far I doubt he'd seen his feet in years, evidence of his wealth and ability to provide. We were working as *porteurs* together, big plastic buckets strapped to our backs, and while I panted along he ambled up and down the rows of vines, laughing and making jokes, occasionally bursting into song. He began his overtures of friendship by offering me the occasional cigarette at the end of a line, always coming out with one of his favourite lines: 'Care to smoke a Gitane – a *Gypsy*?'

Soon he moved on to making derogatory remarks about the French, maybe to see what my reaction would be, and I pointed out that the French were the old enemies of the English, that there was no love lost between us, which had him thinking. Then a week into the *vendange* he suddenly invited me back to the Manouche campfires, as if he'd made up his mind about something. The other men nodded as we arrived and offered a place on a log, and for the first time I shared a small part of their lives, eating their food and afterwards listening to their songs, most of which sounded like laments.

'You know,' Meme told me, 'we Manouche don't trust houses. We think they are a false security. If we lived in a house we'd be worried that the roof would fall onto our heads.'

Chocote was an altogether different kettle of fish. He was the unelected but universally accepted head of the company, a severe but kindly man, I guessed in his mid-forties, with his trademark flat cap. He always wore a sweatshirt under a blue denim jacket and jeans. His face was full and well fed but deeply lined, and his dark brown eyes were deep-set and intense. He had a large grey moustache that all but hid his upper lip, from behind which twinkled gold teeth.

A Spanish Gitano, he was married by arrangement to a Manouche, lovely, soft-hearted Oumlo, and he exuded such a force of character that you couldn't help but hold him in a least a little bit of awe. It was an indication of the force of his personality that he, once an outsider, now commanded respect amongst all Manouche who knew him, and not just in his own company. The mood of the whole camp depended on his mood; anyone with a problem went to Chocote to ask for help. If there was a dispute between families, or even within a family, Chocote would be called upon to pronounce judgement. I never saw anyone answer him back in anger; if he felt compelled to hand out a tongue-lashing the victim just stood, head down, until dismissed. Most of the *rom*, despite being heavy smokers, wouldn't even light up in front of him for fear that he would take it as a sign of disrespect.

The other heads of family included Ghuno's husband Paquili, a tall and handsome but angry-looking man. His eyes were a little too close together, giving him a bit of a squint, and his chest was covered by a tattoo of two fists bound by a chain, with the words *Liberty for my Children* underneath. He actually had two wives, as some Manouche did, which I'll come to. Then there was a brother-in-law of Paquili, Mochi, a short fat man with a high-pitched voice who complained a lot, and finally Roupenho, the youngest, who everyone called 'Mr Kojak' because he was in the habit of shaving his head.

Together our two groups made up almost the entire workforce, something that was to have a dramatic impact. At the beginning of the final week before the *vendange* was due to end, Jean-Pierre's father announced that the Manouche were no longer needed; the harvest could be finished by our group even if it had to be extended for a day or two. He wanted the Manouche off his land sooner rather than later, but it was the wrong call.

That evening I approached a glum-looking Chocote as he sat by the fire with a proposal. He was angry with the patron, those few days' work meant a lot to the company, but he didn't feel they could do anything about it. That was just the way things were, and the Manouche were used to such treatment.

'How about if I tell my people to stop work tomorrow?' I said to him. 'Will you support me?'

'What do you mean?' he replied cautiously.

'We'll have a strike. The patron needs to finish the *vendange*. If we all stop work together we are strong. We started this *vendange* together, so we should finish it together.'

Chocote took his time before responding, looking at me appraisingly from his dark, deep-set eyes. 'Okay, we'll support you. But I hope you are right, that it works; we don't want to lose more work. And we've been coming to this place for years.'

We turned up in the vineyards as usual in the morning, but immediately sent word to Pierre Renaudat that we were stopping work forthwith because of grievances. The Manouche were incredulous; they couldn't imagine any *gadjo*, non-Gypsies, putting their livelihoods at risk to help them, and they promised to also stop work immediately if we were dismissed. If that happened then Tête Rouge could be left with a large number of unpicked grapes. With the rain closing in, any significant delay could be catastrophic.

Pierre Renaudat arrived amongst us, utterly bewildered. Like many in the Bordeaux area, he was a committed Anglophile. He had even joked when he had hired us that he supposed the English would be going on strike, such was England's reputation at the time.

'Why are you doing this? Why are you taking their side against me?' He didn't seem so much angry as irritated and disappointed in me. He was actually a very kindly man, tall and slim with an aristocratic bearing, and he had of course welcomed me into his house as Jean-Pierre's *ami Anglais*.

'It's not about taking sides or being against anyone,' I explained. 'We just feel that after two weeks we should finish together what we started together. And that if anyone is to be sent home, it shouldn't be just because they are Manouche. It doesn't seem fair, especially as they work much faster than us.'

Jean-Pierre's father shook his head and looked up at the sky as if gauging the weather. I think he knew what I was up to. He turned back to me and almost smiled, speaking softly. 'You are young and idealistic, and not a little bit arrogant, but I should have guessed. So be it, then.'

Within an hour we were back at work, and in the event we finished the *vendange* a day early anyway, so Pierre Renaudat didn't lose much. Jean-Pierre wasn't there, he was working in Paris as a photographer, but later when we met again he said he understood and that his father didn't bear any grudge.

Everyone was so happy we seemed to work double-quick, and on the final day, when we had all been paid, we left together, moving to a field surrounded by trees several miles away, where we threw a massive party.

There was a mountain of food – Meme wanted to buy a whole pig to roast over the fire but was restrained – and there were crates of beer and a lake of wine. The women made themselves up beautifully; for the first time I saw them in all their finery, sporting long flowered skirts and gold earrings and necklaces. Even some of the men had made the effort to shave and spruce themselves up a bit.

Several groups of Manouche who I'd not seen before arrived; it was the last coming together of the families before they all dispersed for winter, splitting into small groups again. We ate and danced and sang; it was an outpouring of Manouche pride and emotion. For a while it was wild and threatened to get out of hand, the music blaring from a battery-powered turntable. The dancing was furious until everyone was bathed in sweat.

Then, when the children had finally tired and crept away to their caravans or simply fallen asleep in the nearest pair of arms by the fireside, the mood shifted. Guitars were produced and the men started taking turns to sing, and it became nostalgic, as if we were touched by an inner weariness that spoke not of a few summer months on the road, nor even a lifetime, but of a millennium, the voyages of the Manouche people.

Ernesto sang a beautiful haunting rhumba from his native Brazil, and then Chocote took the guitar to accompany Meme's singing. Chocote's big labourer's fingers were transformed as they danced nimbly around the chords, his spare hand strumming and slapping the wooden guitar in a Spanish flamenco rhythm. Meme was larger than life, his face flushed with wine and effort as he sat bolt upright, eyes closed, and he hung on to long high wavering notes, relating tales from their youth, of the family they had left behind in Valencia and crossing the Pyrenees to escape from Franco's Spain, when there was nothing to eat except potato or orange peelings or even grass, and of their new beginnings in France, of the years since right up until the present day, and he had tears streaming down his face. It was a fitting end to the evening; no one wanted to try to follow a performance like that, and there was hardly a dry eye left amongst those still gathered around the fire's embers.

The following morning we all parted to go our separate ways, but not before Chocote, Meme and Paquili came to me and, in a rare show of affection to an outsider, held me with both hands, giving me an address in Marseille.

'You are one of us now,' Chocote said solemnly, piercing me with those deep dark eyes of his. 'You will be welcome to come and stay and travel with us whenever you want.'

Meme gave me a tiny gold heart, which I attached to my watch. 'It's the heart of the Gypsies,' he said.

'Thank you, I'll come early next year,' I said, becoming emotional again. 'You'll see me sooner than you think.' Then I turned to my Bedford van, where the others in my group were waiting to begin the long drive home.

The *vendange* 1979 with (L-R) Mochi, Chocote, Roupenho, Beudjeu and Casque.

The trusty Beford van with (L-R) Andy, the author, Margeurita and Liz, Dordogne 1979.

Mirabeau

In London I threw myself into work to raise funds, working twelve-hour night shifts at the BBC's Broadcasting House in Portland Place. I hated it, and quickly understood how the BBC had allegedly inspired George Orwell's Ministry of Truth in his prescient novel of the future, *Nineteen Eighty-Four*, even if with supreme irony that didn't stop them putting up a statue of him outside their headquarters. I was staying with an old school friend called Eddy Babbage in his house in Stockwell in the south of London, but I rarely saw anyone. I worked by night and slept by day, but it meant I didn't spend much and the money was okay.

By Christmas I had enough funds to trade in my trusty old Bedford van and bought a much newer VW camper from some Australian travellers in the Aldwych, on the north side of Waterloo Bridge, which at that time was a sort of *ad hoc* street market for all sorts of vehicles. I fitted it out with a bed and cupboards, sprayed it silver and cut windows into the roof. It seemed like a great upgrade at the time, but it was to prove to be a mistake.

I was ready well before spring and prepared for the 700-mile drive to Marseille, packing clothes and a sleeping bag, with plenty of spare underwear. I had stocked up on English tea, baked beans, corned beef, sugar and tinned milk, along with assorted pots and pans. I also had two 35mm cameras and a dozen rolls of film.

'You're mad,' Eddy said on the day of my departure. 'They'll probably rob you blind, and what are you going to do there anyway? You're not one of them, never will be.'

'I'll be fine,' I told him. 'If it doesn't work out I can always come back, but if I don't go I'll never forgive myself; I'll always be wondering about what might have been. I'll send you a *Poste Restante* address where you can contact me.'

'Well, good luck,' he said, shaking my hand. 'Stay in touch.' Then I crunched the VW into gear and headed for Dover.

Being back on the road after the months of night shifts was exhilarating. On the crossing from Dover I stayed on deck the whole way, watching the famous white cliffs fade into the distance and looking at the churning water in the ship's wake while breathing in the fresh salty air.

Once in France I avoided the expensive motorways and toll roads, and stuck to the *Routes Nationales*. I headed first towards Reims, then on to Dijon and Lyon, Valence, and on towards Avignon, either pulling into a roadside layby to sleep or on a couple of occasions stopping in campsites which offered decent hot showers and toilets. I'm a slow driver and the VW wasn't the fastest anyway, so it wasn't until early on the morning of the fifth day that I saw Marseille sprawled by the sea below and descended towards the city from the surrounding hills.

I had the address that Meme had given me, but each time I stopped to ask for further directions, at a café or taxi rank, I got curious looks, usually a shrug as well, and was pointed further and further in the direction of the docks. It was there, moving slowly along the coastal road with the sea and empty containers and discarded tyres on one side, that on a patch of wasteland on the other side I spotted a large number of caravans and Peugeot and Saviem vans, with a crude hand-painted sign saying *Welcome to Mirabeau* nailed to a post. I had arrived.

I turned in cautiously, scrawny dogs snapping at the VW's wheels and setting up a cacophony of barking and growls until stones were thrown and they scampered yelping away. Fortunately Chocote's company occupied a large patch just inside the entrance, on the left-hand side, and they recognised me immediately, surrounding the van and shouting excitedly. They guided me to a spot alongside Chocote's and Oumlo's caravan, where I finally emerged to warm embraces.

Elsewhere in the camp, but divided by invisible boundaries, were groups of Jenische who had mainly come from Germany, Yugoslav Romanies, Spanish Gitanos and other travellers of uncertain origin, about 200 people in all, of which Chocote's company numbered thirty or forty people spanning up to four generations from half a dozen families.

Chocote was especially welcoming, making me his personal guest and according me full *rom* or adult status even though I was unmarried. Oumlo, helped by Ghuno and the other women, laid on a feast that first night and the guitars came out around the braziers. Everyone was there, Mochi, Paquili, Roupenho and others who I knew less well such as Chiclo, Matzo and Narte. The children formed a circle and clapped along to the songs while I just soaked it up, grinning like an idiot, staring at the stars and knowing that making the journey had been the right move. But there was no Meme.

'Where's Meme?' I asked Chocote. 'Why is he not here?'

'We'll go and see him soon,' he replied enigmatically. 'He's not far away, but he doesn't stay at Mirabeau. You will see him soon.'

From then on Chocote treated me almost as one of his own sons, and his eldest son, Beudjeu, soon became one of my best friends amongst the Manouche. We'd go out in his Peugeot van on an almost daily basis to rummage through the local municipal rubbish tips. Anything was better than sitting all day in the dust and dirt of the ironically named Mirabeau: 'beautiful view'.

We'd set off early, by 6am, wanting to be the first to hit the dumps and grab any scrap left by the disposal trucks the previous evening – first gets all and second gets nothing. The Manouche knew everything of any possible value and picked over the tips carefully, experts at living off the garbage of society. Sometimes we would drive fifty or even a hundred miles in an outing if scrap was scarce, passing the French peasants scratching away at their tiny plots of land.

'Stupid peasants,' Beudjeu would laugh, 'killing themselves for nothing. We Manouche are smarter than that; we don't work for our living.'

He was right in a way. Our 'working' day rarely stretched beyond midday, when it was time for lunch, and was hardly strenuous. But it wasn't really something anyone would aspire to either. It's a strange feeling, searching through other people's waste for survival, and incredible what you can find: nearly new clothes and shoes, children's toys galore and even food, dumped because the sell-by date has passed by a day or two.

We hit the jackpot once at a time when money was at zero; we didn't even have enough to buy food for an evening meal except a watery soup. We were sitting listlessly in the dust of Mirabeau as the sun started to sink, thinking of nothing very much except how hungry we were, when Beudjeu rose.

'I've still got some petrol in my van; let's see what we can find,' he said, looking at me.

Beudjeu was about my age, a few years younger but more worldly-wise in many ways, lean but strong, with black hair and a wispy beard. He was often serious, maybe part of the burden of being Chocote's son, but also had a wicked sense of humour. He was about the only one in the company who could read and write without much difficulty, even if his spelling was entirely phonetic and bore little resemblance to actual French words.

We drove into the gathering dusk, visiting first one dump, then another and another, in a fruitless search for something of value. As darkness fell we came to the fourth rubbish tip on our circuit just as a large van started unloading a veritable feast – cakes, biscuits, crisps, tinned milk even, all a day or two past their sell-by date, and as fast as the guys unloaded the van, we grabbed the lot, transferring it to the back of the Peugeot.

By the time our yellow headlights swept back into Mirabeau, Chocote was already organising a search party; we'd been gone too long and hunger had made everyone edgy. But anxiety quickly turned to delight when we revealed our treasure, and that night we stuffed ourselves with milky coffee and cakes and wondered about the people who threw away such things.

Another day Beudjeu made a mistake. He found the hull of a burnt-out car at a scrap heap and wasted no time in starting to break it down, salvaging anything of value. The police arrived as he was at it, demanding papers, conducting a search, the usual. It turned out the car was stolen and Beudjeu became suspect number one. It was obvious he was just scavenging, but it still cost him a hefty fine.

Mostly life at Mirabeau had little to recommend it; it was just somewhere warm and generally dry where the company could pass the winter before the travelling season came around again. There was little comfort apart from a couple of pumps which provided water. For our morning toilet we'd cross the road to squat amongst the containers and piles of old tyres – and we never went alone. For security even this simple act was conducted in pairs, and we squatted within hailing distance of each other.

From the outside Mirabeau looked like a huge rubbish tip, which is more or less what it was, except with humans living in it. There were caravans and rotting buses and vans converted to homes wedged between piles of scrap metal and other junk, with discarded plastic bags and cardboard boxes, bottles and cans strewn around. Inside, the caravans were immaculate, or most of them were, but no one took care of the outside, even if Chocote did mark out his own little front yard with wire fencing which was kept clean, and where he could sit by his brazier in peace. The children were covered in a black dust from dawn to dusk, when they were stood under a pump and scrubbed. It looked uninviting, but the warmth of the people made up for the physical discomforts, and after a while I got used to it; it was 'home'.

The different groups of Gypsies hardly mixed at all, except for when the Yugoslav Romanies, the most colourful of all the groupings with their women in long printed skirts and headscarves, held one of their feast days, such as on St George's Day, the day of their patron saint, or, curiously, on Armistice Day. Then we'd all join in and pass the afternoon with music, food and, of course, wine, served out of litre plastic bottles.

Outside visitors were, not surprisingly, few and far between, apart from the occasional doctor, social worker or other do-gooder. The exception was when a ship docked from China, and groups of Chinese sailors would saunter through the site with no apparent qualms. They seemed as fascinated by us as we were by them, always in groups of four or five and in matching Mao pyjama suits. Maybe it satisfied them to see such squalor, as if it vindicated their own system and beliefs, for here was living evidence of the oppressed in the capitalist world. And the Manouche love a bit of role playing if it's good for a laugh.

'Hey, look! Five Bruce Lees come to take a look at the cannibal barbarians!' someone shouted as a group of Chinese entered the camp once. Several of the Gypsy youths leapt up and down, hooting and scratching, while others looked on and laughed, but as usual the sailors' faces remained like masks, expressionless. Until some of the children went too far. The Manouche children implicitly believed everything they saw in the movies and were convinced that all Chinese were martial arts masters, so they teased the sailors with kung fu antics from a safe distance, and then one threw a bottle which landed just in front of the visiting group. A burly sailor immediately stepped forward, taking up a classic kung fu stance and growling. There was the sound of several caravan doors being slammed shut, followed by silence. There was not a Gypsy in sight, and it stayed that way until the Chinese had finished their tour and left the site.

For the most part, though, there was too much inactivity in Marseille. We couldn't hunt or fish in the city like in the countryside, and anyway most Manouche avoided going beyond the camp limits on foot for fear of harassment from the police, who they called the *schmidt* or *klistey*. I have this thing about walking: I need to do it every day, a compulsion that was always a complete mystery to the rest of the company, who regarded walking as a discomfort to be undertaken only in extreme necessity. It proved their point to them when one night my walking ended in a brush with the law.

I'd made my way through the dark streets around the docks to the nearest working telephone kiosk about a mile away, enjoying the evening cool, and decided to call home.

I'd just started talking when the kiosk door was yanked open and a hand cut my call off.

'What the fuck?'

A squat unsmiling man with a black leather coat and pencil moustache faced me, one hand on his hip, the other outstretched towards me, demanding my papers. Across the road the blue light of a police van turned lazily.

'You just cost me two Francs, what do you think you're doing?' I demanded.

'Give me your papers, tell me what you're doing here.'

'Making a fucking phone call, what does it look like?'

'You were robbing the box.'

'You're crazy.'

'Last time, show me your papers.'

'Bullshit, show me *your* papers, how do I even know you're a cop?'

Leather Coat dragged me violently into the street, and one of his heavies ran over and held a gun to my head as I was frisked.

They found nothing; I didn't even have any identity papers except for my passport, which was back in my van, and in France that's not good. They shoved me into the back of their van and radioed in that they were bringing in a 'suspect'.

Just then, and right on time, Beudjeu and one of his younger brothers, Blon, arrived in the Peugeot. They too were given a thorough search and their papers were checked. All were in order and Beudjeu explained that I was a foreigner, a tourist on holiday, and staying with them. You could see the distaste in the police's faces, but they eventually seemed to decide I could be more trouble than it was worth, and I was released with a sharp warning that it was ten in the evening, too late to be out making phone calls.

'Watch your step,' said Leather Coat before they drove away.

'Where did you come from?' I asked Beudjeu as we clambered into the Peugeot.

'We were behind you all the way, just making sure you were okay.'

'Thanks. I thought I was headed for the cells, or something worse. I mean, what was that with the gun?'

'Next time maybe it's better you don't ask the *klistey* for their ID,' he said with a grin. Which was the big joke in Mirabeau the next day when the story had spread.

19

While most of us spent at least part of the day out hunting for scrap and iron, others did as little as possible, people like Mochi and Paquili. Mochi was almost completely round with small eyes; his fat belly hung over his belt, which was pulled tight above short legs, and we called him *pesi balo*, 'fat pig', which he thought was funny. He never seemed to do anything except tinker with his car, a Peugeot 404, a Manouche favourite, and argue with his wife Sarah. Paquili on the other hand said he was going to get rich on social security by having fifteen children, and with two wives and eleven kids he was already well on the way. He was a brother-in-law to Chocote, tall from some German blood somewhere, he said, and good-looking when he wasn't scowling about something or other, which he did quite a lot. He slept latest of all, rising well after nine in the morning. He would occasionally spray paint vans or cars or do odd mechanical jobs, both of which he was very gifted at, but mostly he did nothing very much except avoiding Ghuno and his second wife Nina, which was an occupation in itself.

The hardest workers of all amongst the Manouche are of course the women. The duties of men and women are strictly divided. The Manouche are a very conservative people, living within a very tight and closed world. At least it was then. When every one of your actions has a direct impact on the group, maybe the rules need to be more rigid. When you are not alone in anything you do and there is no privacy, then it only works if everyone belongs, knows his or her duties and respects the status quo. Or so it seemed at the time.

While the status quo for the men meant cruising in their vans for scrap or hanging out at Mirabeau drinking coffee and smoking, for the women it meant shopping for food twice a day (without refrigeration nothing was stored), collecting water in urns from one of the pumps or roadside taps outside, washing clothes, cooking, cleaning already spotless caravans and keeping an eye on the children. Even heavily pregnant women carried on hefting buckets of water and scrubbing clothes on an old board before somehow also serving up lunch and dinner on time.

Oumlo beat them all. She was a tall, slender woman who always held herself upright, with dyed blond hair and large doe eyes, and oozed kindness. She kept herself busy from early morning until midnight, washing the caravan floor and polishing all the brass and silver several times a day, dusting the shelves, feeding Chocote and their children – apart from Beudjeu and Blon they also had two younger sons, Niglo and Pepite – and generally making sure that the family plot was always the best kept in Mirabeau by a country mile.

On the insides most caravans gleamed. Ghuno's was another that was always cleaner than clean. At any time of the day there were three or four people dropping by for some comfort, gossip and a coffee from the jug that simmered all day. Despite this Ghuno still managed all the other chores while also coping with four children born deaf mutes. Young Bianca, mature beyond her thirteen years, also helped a lot. Ghuno and Paquili were first cousins, which many said explained why so many of their seven children were born like that.

Paquili had taken a second wife, the mischievous and slovenly red-haired Nina. Polygamy isn't common amongst the Manouche, but nor is it frowned upon in circumstances like Paquili's. But Ghuno never forgave him, refusing to sleep with him again and only reluctantly allowing him into their caravan for a coffee now and then. He slept with Nina in his big white Mercedes van. Ghuno's contempt was picked up by their children and held against Paquili, and often when he was drunk he would take himself off to a quiet corner and cry for hours on end.

'He has sickness of the heart,' Chocote said.

left: Blon (on left) and Beudjeu, Mirabeau 1980.

below: Yugoslav Romanies, Mirabeau.

Shopping

The French distrust the Manouche as Gypsies are distrusted everywhere, but crime wasn't rife amongst our company or others at Mirabeau, even if Marseille was more tempting than the countryside. The North African gangs, mostly Algerians or Tunisians, were more serious, especially the ones who were packed into the huge housing estates to the north of the city. These had been built after World War II when the French empire had collapsed to house the white settlers who fled home, but had since been taken over by the masses of North African immigrants, many of whom lived off crime, mostly drugs, and were said to be armed to the teeth. We stayed well clear of them.

The Manouche tended to keep themselves to themselves and at the most indulged in petty theft, pilfering from shops or stealing cars for joyrides. Sometimes twelve- or thirteen-year-olds drove into the camp in big BMWs or Mercedes, puffed up with pride, before quickly disappearing again to dump the car somewhere well away from Mirabeau.

But nor did the Manouche look a gift horse in the mouth. A *gadjo* parked his brand new Simca right outside Mirabeau and walked off into the night. It's hard to imagine what he thought would happen; it was like leaving a raw steak in front of a pack of hyenas. When he came back the next morning it was gutted, the shell up on bricks.

'Hey!' he shouted at some of the children. 'Who did this?' He walked angrily towards them, fists clenched, but stopped when several *rom* moved forwards and looked at him without expression, arms folded across their chests and legs apart. 'Shit, shit, shit!' the man shouted before turning on his heel and marching off. He probably had insurance, so we didn't see the problem. He'd asked for it, really; that was how we saw it.

Shoplifting was the exclusive domain of the women. Young girls were taught the tricks of the trade by their mothers, there was a lot of role playing, and the women would have a few trial runs at the camp before a real outing.

I met Paquili's second wife Nina and two other women, Tac-Tac and Nanine, on their way to the shops as I returned from a walk one day, and against all convention insisted I accompany them to help carry things home.

'You won't *do* anything?' Tac-Tac didn't look too happy about it.

'What do you mean?'

'I mean just, well, shopping is for women.'

'I won't interfere, I promise, just help you carry the shopping back.'

Inside the cramped mini-market the women kept throwing me furtive looks, picking up items and examining them before putting them back on the shelves, and a few minutes later picking up the same thing and repeating the process.

'I think I smell something in here; is it you, woman?' Nanine said to the shopkeeper, who looked back, bemused. 'Oh, I'm sorry, you don't speak Manouche, do you?' Switching into French, 'I was just saying how lovely your dress is.'

Nina called me to a far corner of the shop to ask the price of some fruits.

'But you can read the label yourself.'

Nina looked at me helplessly. They wanted to distract me but were becoming so nervous the shopkeeper was getting suspicious.

'You buying or just looking?' She was a florid-faced woman with meaty arms who didn't seem the kind to ask too many questions first.

In an instant I realised the Manouche women were *my* distraction, made a quick tour of the shop, paid for some matches and left.

It wasn't long before Nina, Tac-Tac and Nanine also came out, glum-faced. They'd been in the shop too long and had attracted too much attention to try anything stupid and had left empty-handed.

I rejoined them. 'Good hunting?'

'What do you mean?' Nina was looking grumpy.

'I mean what were all those games about? Were you thinking to fool me and the *gadje*' – the feminine form of *gadjo* – 'at the same time?'

'We didn't do anything.'

'No, but you made it easy for me.' From inside my jacket I produced a half-bottle of vodka and another of rum and dropped them into Nina's shopping bag. 'I felt like a drink.'

There was a moment's stunned silence, and then they all burst into laughter. 'We didn't even see you, not a thing!'

'The shopkeeper was looking at you and you were looking at her.'

Did I feel bad? Yes and no. We were outsiders; the *gadjo* were there for the taking, but not in a big way. I wouldn't know where to find it, but if that shop is still there I'd happily pay with interest.

Apart from the shopping and scrap work, few Manouche ventured outside Mirabeau, especially at night. The family was their world; they had no stake in anything outside the camp; they were wary about the outside even if there was nothing to do inside. But doing nothing isn't as easy as it sounds.

Mirabeau offered little shade and often a hot wind blew over from North Africa, covering everything and everyone with gritty dust. Tempers would fray. Disputes broke out almost daily but rarely came to blows; invariably the antagonists would be related in some way, and fighting with family broke all the rules.

A furious squabble amongst a group of Jenische, men and women, ended with one of the men slashing himself across his chest with a hunting knife; there was plenty of blood but it looked worse than it was. And one night everyone was woken by the sound of smashing glass; Tac-Tac's husband Koki, a young Spanish Gitano who was part of our group, was using a baseball bat in a drunken rage to shatter every window in his caravan and car.

'I just had to let it out,' he said the next day as he looked at the broken remains of his home.

Any diversion was welcome. Mirabeau was emptied by the sight of an ancient one-legged man on crutches pulling himself along the adjoining road, dragging his belongings behind him in a large hessian sack. His clothes were ragged and dirty and his long grey hair was tied back in a ponytail. He was clearly a traveller of some sort and the Gypsies were agog.

'Who are you?' Paquili called out.

'I'm no one.' He had a strange accent and wheezed a lot. Excited conversation ensued. He said he'd travelled everywhere in the world and claimed to speak half a dozen languages, including Russian.

'Where are you going now?'

'I think the city centre, but I'll know when I get there.'

Immediately half a dozen hands shot up with offers of a lift, but they were all firmly declined.

The next morning Beudjeu and I headed towards downtown Marseille and after just a couple of miles found the old man still hauling himself along the road, painfully slowly. He'd obviously slept out in the open.

'Come on, we'll give you a lift,' Beudjeu said to him.

He squinted up and shook his head. 'Thank you, but I'm not even sure where I'm going, so it's fine like this.'

We drove on, making for a municipal dump, shaking our heads in wonder. 'Who do you think he is?' Beudjeu asked.

'No idea. A loner down on his luck, I guess.'

'But where's his family?'

'Maybe he hasn't got one, or maybe he left them.'

That was a concept that Beudjeu just couldn't understand.

Another problem in the city was watching the children. They were as restless as anyone with the constant confinement to camp, and it wasn't unusual to see some toddler heading single-mindedly towards the heavy traffic thundering by outside, drawn by the forbidden, before one of the women ran to scoop him or her up. The Manouche also worried excessively about their children being abducted and mistreated by the *gadjo*, which was ironic given the *gadjo*'s own fixed narrative about Gypsies stealing children.

'It's what they think, but it's impossible,' Chocote said, whittling a

26

piece of wood. 'For us, children are sacred. We would never inflict that sort of suffering on a parent by taking a child. They are innocents. Children are special to us.'

Sitting around the brazier one night talking softly, the night was suddenly torn by a horrible scream, and another. And then we heard the dog, not barking but a deep-throated primaeval growling as it tore at something. Paquili, Beudjeu and Narte ran towards the noise, which was coming from a scrapyard adjacent to Mirabeau, and scaled the fence. There was shouting and the sound of scuffling, and then a dull thud and the dog went silent. A *gadjo* started shouting as our men ran back, Paquili with a young boy in his arms, limp, bloodied, and too frightened to cry in more than gulping sobs.

It was sixteen-year-old Niglo, a nephew of Mochi who'd slipped unnoticed through the fence into the yard for who knew what reason, maybe just because it was out of bounds. The guard, an older *gadjo* of fifty or sixty, scrawny and always angry at the world, had loosed his German shepherd on the boy. Paquili and the others had arrived as the man was about to lock dog and boy into a wooden shack together, and he could have done it and got away with it, because Niglo was trespassing.

Niglo would have been savaged to death, but Beudjeu had grabbed an iron bar and stove the dog's head in before Paquili lifted Niglo up and they fled.

The boy would carry terrible scars for the rest of his life; one leg was badly chewed and was bleeding heavily. No ambulance was called; instead Ghuno and Oumlo cleaned the wound as best they could and poured on antiseptic, then bound it tightly with clean bandages, but he would always walk with a severe limp. Clearly not everyone thought children were sacred, especially if they were Manouche children.

Meme

The winters always drifted by much too slowly in the same routine, scrap and iron forays, lunch, dinner, and a lot of sitting around. Christmases came and went quietly, there was no churchgoing (the Manouche have their own saints and devils), but the New Year was greeted noisily in the usual fashion with food, wine and music. As each dusk fell, women wailed for their children to be washed or their menfolk to come for food, each call distinct in its own tone or pitch and easily identifiable throughout the camp for its intended recipient. Fires dotted the site: not the grand log fires that we had in the country, but makeshift braziers with poor-quality wood and pallets taken from the tips.

Chocote used some disused wood and copper to fashion a wall hanging of an artificial fountain which he gave to me, and then he did an intricate crayon drawing on the back of some wallpaper showing a Manouche camp by the river which separated them from the *gadjo* town on the other side. In the picture there is someone fishing, and another with a sack of hedgehogs, a line of washing, dogs, the fires with women roasting hedgehogs on spits, someone weaving cane baskets, someone relieving themselves in the trees, children fetching pails of water, horses, and four horse-drawn caravans. It's a romantic scene of nature and freedom and peace and tranquillity, while across the river the *gadjo* houses sit in a miserable cluster. It still hangs in my house.

Money was always tight and the evening meals were usually sparse, often spicy *merguez* sausages from the Arab markets cooked over the open fire, eaten between hunks of baguette and washed down with hot, milky coffee.

When spring finally approached and the days grew hotter, the evenings were a time for a collective sigh of relief as cool air washed over the site. A guitar might be heard and people would wander in its general direction, going from fire to fire, from caravan to caravan. There was no standing on ceremony; you could enter a caravan, take a cup of coffee and leave without a word if you wanted; everyone was family. Some watched television, others sat by the fires smoking silently as the freight trains rattled by across the road. They were waiting.

The great Manouche festival of Les Saintes-Maries-de-la-Mer in the Camargue at the end of May marked the renewal of the travelling season, just as the *vendange* marked its end. Excitement rippled through the camp; the talk was of nothing else. There were new paint jobs for cars and caravans, a bit of wallpaper here and there inside, and engines were serviced and checked. But there was a dark cloud too.

While the travelling season beckoned, there were those who said its time was past. I'd been badgering Chocote for news of Meme, who was still nowhere to be seen, but the answers were always evasive.

'We'll see him soon,' Chocote would say. 'He's busy.'

Until one day, several weeks after I'd arrived that first year with them, Chocote summoned me and Beudjeu and told us to join him in his van.

'Let's go and see Meme,' he said.

'Where is he? Why isn't he at Mirabeau?'

'You will see,' was all Chocote said with a serious look, which made me wonder if Meme was in some kind of trouble.

He wasn't, but shockingly it seemed that Meme's lament at the end of the previous *vendange* was to be his last, as he had announced he was to work the municipal dumps all year. He had moved with his wife and ten children into a dingy twelve-storey apartment block shared by other Manouche and North Africans, mostly from the Maghreb. His apartment was halfway up the block, the lifts didn't work, and as Chocote, Beudjeu and I slowly climbed the stairs I felt full of foreboding, although I couldn't explain why.

The stairwells might have been dank and reeking of piss, but inside Meme's apartment everything was pristine. Meme gave us all a huge bear hug and ushered us in. The apartment was decorated with all the knick-knacks you'd find inside the caravans. Madonnas and good luck charms vied with copper fountains, a hunting rifle and shelves of cups and saucers and china vases. But pride of place went to an oversized wall-mounted television which Meme said was on from morning until late at night. It spewed out a litany of turgid junk while he offered us small bowls of thick sweet black coffee in the Manouche way, and then in a departure from custom threw open an impressively stocked drinks cabinet and took out a bottle of brandy, which we declined.

'The *gadjo* threatened to put me in prison if my children didn't go to school, so what can I do? I'll go back on the road when they finish school.'

'You told me you'd never live in a house in case the roof fell on your head, and now you're in an apartment block!' I showed him the small gold heart he'd given me.

Meme shrugged sadly, half-filling a tumbler with brandy. It didn't seem to be his first of the day.

'Your children will be taught in a different way, they won't know the ways of the road any more, they won't know how to survive off the land.'

'They will have a better future.'

'Will they?'

'What can I do? There is no choice.' Meme hunched over the table, looking down at his half-empty glass.

After a while no one knew what to say any more and Chocote, Beudjeu and I took our leave.

'You see?' Chocote took me by the arm. 'Do you see how quickly it's happening? The children are already no longer like us, they watch television and speak French.' The same was to happen to Chocote as well, but perhaps less brutally.

That evening there was an animated discussion about the merits of bowing to the seeming inevitable and giving up the travelling life.

'It's getting harder to live off the land,' Chocote the pragmatist said. 'It means weaving baskets all day and going door to door for a pittance, fishing or hunting hedgehogs. Sometimes we don't even know where the next meal is coming from. In twenty years hardly any of us will be living in caravans.'

Everyone around the fire listened in respectful silence, mulling over his words. We knew what he was thinking. Just a hundred yards along the road the local authorities had cleared another wasteland and were building about forty small one-room houses in two rows divided by a road. They'd be ready in midsummer and the social workers had been around a lot trying to persuade the Gypsies to move. They were promised hot and cold water, a toilet, kitchenette and a large room with a mezzanine, upstairs for sleeping and downstairs for eating. The Gypsies were also told they could keep their caravans and park them up by the houses, and they would be able to trade in their nomad papers for real French identity papers.

Paquili stood up. 'I travel because I'm a true Manouche,' he said. 'If I stay in a house I get sick. The road is in my blood.'

Everyone nodded agreement with that, Chocote too, even if in his heart he knew Paquili's travelling days were also likely to be numbered.

Chocote was one of the few Manouche in the company who seemed able to think in the abstract. Most of them only thought about what was, not what might be. Such as when Nina came back from the shops and told me she'd only paid 1.80 francs a kilo for potatoes, when they were 2.70 francs further up the road.

'Why the difference?'

'Because they're more expensive up the road.'

'Yes, but why?'

'Because they cost more.'

It wasn't important why the potatoes cost so much more in one place than the other, it was a fact, so why waste time trying to reason it?

I spent many hours with Chocote discussing what the future might hold and he would become emotional and nostalgic, as if he were carrying a deep sadness.

'Sometimes I find myself crying in my sleep,' he said.

He was proud of being Manouche; he said they could laugh in the face of adversity and live off their wits, unlike the *gadjo*, and that it was important to live for the day rather than for some distant point in the future that may never arrive. But he was also resigned to the changes that were taking place, the gradual erosion of their culture and ways, accepting them with the fatalistic shrug with which the Manouche tend to accept all burdens.

'Maybe it'll take another two generations,' he said. 'Then we could all be in houses. Maybe we are seeing the last generation of travelling Manouche growing up, but that's the way it is.'

'Surely it doesn't have to be like that?'

'The *gadjo* want us settled, they don't want us travelling any more, what can we do?' Chocote sighed sadly, shrugged, and looked at me with his dark penetrating eyes.

Customs were already fading. Everyone still spat regularly into the heart of the fire, but no one knew why they did it any more. Other superstitions, though, especially surrounding Beng, the devil, remained very much alive, even if they played a smaller part in city life than in the country.

Oumlo and Chocote.

Chocote crafting a copper water fountain.

Les Saintes

After the weeks of excited anticipation, the annual pilgrimage to Les Saintes-Maries-de-la-Mer arrived suddenly. We were eager to get going, like racehorses who'd been kept cooped up for too long. Driving in convoy was like making a statement: *We are Manouche, free to travel where we want with the wind at our backs.*

It should have been only a two-hour run from Marseille along the coast towards Spain, but for us moving in a group it took twice that. Paquili took the lead in his white Mercedes as Chocote rarely went to Les Saintes any more.

'Too many *gadjo* tourists,' he said. 'It's not the same any more, or maybe I'm just too long in the tooth.'

Others joked that he didn't want to spend his money, that he wouldn't travel more than a hundred yards without a wad of notes as thick as a brick for security. But he promised to join us for the journey north when Les Saintes was over.

We drove off in a frenzy, fifty or sixty miles an hour with the caravans swaying crazily behind until we all became separated, and Paquili eventually pulled into a layby where we could regroup and take coffee.

The sight that greeted us at Les Saintes was enough to make the breast of any Manouche swell with pride. Thousands were camped out under the burning sun, guitars putting out the familiar flamenco rhythm on every street corner, fires dotting the landscape as if it were some sort of mediaeval army, hundreds of car cassette players blaring out Manolo or Manitas de Plata. Here we were no longer outsiders, here we belonged.

We laid claim to a patch of disused land and arranged our cars, vans and caravans in a circle, and a foraging party set off to search for wood. A fire was soon going and pots of coffee began to boil. I wandered off with Beudjeu and Blon to look at the other caravans. Some were fantastically wealthy with beautiful hand paintings of Madonnas and crosses and suns and stars on the sides, and huge American cars parked alongside. And Chocote was right about the tourists; there were almost as many of them as Gypsies, loaded down with cameras that clicked constantly.

'I hate them,' Beudjeu muttered. 'They make me feel like an animal in a zoo. How would they like it?'

Among them was Eddy from London, nicknamed the Bear because of his huge frame and habit of wearing a sheepskin coat, and with him was his new Sardinian wife, Theresa. He'd been working on some film documentary in the Ardèche which had gone bust, and they came to pitch a tent with us for a couple of days.

'It's amazing, everyone is so warm, so welcoming,' Eddy said. 'Now I think I understand why you came.'

'Yes, it's like family already, but don't be mistaken; they welcome you because you're with me, but you wouldn't want to camp out here on your own. They probably really would rob you blind, like you thought they'd do to me.' I smiled, reminding him of our conversation when I'd left London the first time to join the Manouche.

'Not a lot of comfort, though. Theresa's idea of roughing it is a five-star hotel,' he remarked wryly.

'You get used to it; physical comfort isn't everything. You know it's going to be hard for me to leave these guys one day. Or maybe I'll stay.'

'You can't go native!' Eddy shook his head and laughed.

'*Dobre tume Romale!*' A young man darted out of the crowd and embraced Beudjeu and Blon; he was a distant cousin.

'*Nais tuke,*' Beudjeu responded, happy to see him, and hand in hand they walked with me and Blon trailing behind to the cousin's nearby caravan, where we took coffee.

With thousands of people milling about, Les Saintes was a scene of complete confusion, but somewhere amidst the chaos there was a sort of order. We bought some wine and returned to our camp for dinner, where some were already getting drunk after polishing off most of a bottle of whisky. Dinner was somehow postponed and finally forgotten as the wine was passed around, until by nightfall we were reeling but still ready for an evening out and wandered in a group back to the town.

After an hour or so of pushing and shoving our way through streets packed with dancing, singing, violin- and guitar-playing Gypsies and tourists, Paquili and Mochi spotted a group of *gadjo* hitchhikers who'd pitched their tents on open ground instead of in one of the private campsites, and decided to have some fun. They drew knives and sliced the ropes of the tents with the *gadjo* inside, muffling laughter. They were just turning to run when one of the residents, a big Scandinavian-looking youth with long curly blond hair, scrambled clear of the wreckage of his tent wearing just his underpants and lunged at Mochi, almost pushing him to the ground.

'What are you doing? You have to pay me for that!'

Paquili and Mochi advanced on him and pinned him to the ground. He started to struggle, but they still had knives out, which was enough to convince him to lie quietly while they sheared his locks.

'That wasn't really necessary, was it?' I said back at camp.

'This is our place. All year round we are pushed about, but not here,' Paquili said grimly, and Mochi giggled his high-pitched laugh.

The next day was Saint Sara's day, *Sara Kalou*, Black Sara, who is the patron saint of the Manouche. Some said the Camargue was the place where migrating Gypsies coming up from Spain met others following the route along the northern Mediterranean, which was why the festival was held there every year. Sara's statue was dark-skinned and dressed in beautiful embroidered silks, and we followed the escort of horsemen as she was carried about a mile to the beach and immersed in the water for the washing away of sins. At the front a priest with a microphone like some sort of Pied Piper led the thousands of Gypsies and tourists in a snake to the water's edge, camera crews jostling for space, the cameras like machine guns.

'What's happening?'

'Did you see anything?'

'Did you get a picture?'

It was pandemonium, but already the snake with Saint Sara at its head was turning and making its way back towards the church. Inside it was more chaos, there were just too many people and the tourists were taking too much space, but this was a special day for baptisms. Les Saintes is considered lucky for a baptism by the Manouche and this time Paquili was naming his latest son after me, the first Nigel in the company, although they pronounced it *Nadjo*.

We sat with the priest in his office, with half a dozen other families who were having children baptised, and he explained how the ceremony would go. A baptism is one of the few times you will see the Manouche entering a church. They are nominally Catholics in France, but mostly because they don't need religious persecution added to all of the rest. Otherwise they follow their own saints and spirits.

When the priest was done we followed him back inside the church, one of the Manouche holding aloft a lurid painting of Jesus with dark lines on his face and flames coming from his hair, and Paquili and another father carrying bowls of anointed water. The ceremony passed in a blur, blinding white lights popping as television crews and flash camera operators pushed aside parents to get a better angle, guitars still playing somewhere, the priest chanting into his microphone. And then it was over and we made our way back to the camp where a huge bowl of paella was waiting, yellow rice, chicken, mussels, prawns, and a case of beer.

An Italian tourist who claimed to know Manolo parked an enormous camper van alongside us; it had six beds, a shower, fridge, freezer and even a toilet. None of our company had seen anything like it before.

'You really know Manolo?' Koki asked in awe. He was one of our best guitarists, a handsome young man, still in his twenties, with straight jet-black hair and long eyelashes, a thin beard and black eyes. Manolo was in a class of his own when it came to music as far as the Manouche were concerned; he was, after all, a Gitano himself.

'Sure I know him; I met him a couple of times.' The Italian was a slim, dapper man, wearing clean jeans and a yellow cashmere pullover, salt and pepper hair pulled back from his forehead and dark eyes flicking everywhere like a crow's as he accepted coffee and a hunk of salami with bread. We couldn't work out what he was doing there and why he was by himself in such a huge van.

'Where?'

'In Italy, in Milano. He was performing there; it was magnificent!'

Nina's mother Sarah turned her back to the fire. 'Typical *gadjo*. You see how much comfort he can afford for himself, yet he comes here to eat our food.'

He left soon enough, back to his starship which roared into life and left in a cloud of dust, probably to park somewhere safer for the night. Maybe he'd just wanted to indulge in a little Gypsy experience, something to tell the folks back home.

The next morning the mood was fractious. Women shouted at their menfolk, who were mostly hungover and ignored them, while fifteen-year-old Pantoon, who'd managed to lose his virginity with a *gadje* the night before, beamed like a Cheshire cat.

We packed and left one by one, back to Mirabeau for a few days to get organised for the bigger journey north.

'It was better last year,' Mochi proclaimed in his high-pitched voice.

'You say that every year,' Paquili grunted as he hitched Ghuno's caravan to his Mercedes van. Once again Chocote had been proved wisest in staying at home.

Les Saintes-Maries-de-la-Mer.

The Limousin

W̶e expected to be in Mirabeau for just two or three days to get ready for the drive north to the Limousin region in the centre of France, but it turned into more than a week because while we'd been gone Chocote had after all taken an option on one of the houses, and Paquili's parents took the house next door, saying they were just too tired to travel any more.

Ghuno's brother Chiclo, meaning 'little bird', a scrawny man with long curly hair and a beaked nose beneath a cowboy hat, shrugged. 'Well, I don't want to live like a peasant.'

'No, I don't think can l live in a house either,' Paquili said, but Roupenho, Koki and a brother of Paquili, Matzo, Pantoon's father, also opted to take houses. Oumlo was deeply sad; she yearned for the open road and had little enthusiasm for the idea of life in a house, but she was duty-bound to Chocote. Beudjeu too felt duty-bound to stay and help Chocote with the move, and he stayed in his caravan at Mirabeau. All promised to join us in the late summer, in time for the *vendange*, but it was an emotional farewell on both sides when our convoy of five vehicles finally pulled out early one morning. Everyone knew that a momentous change had taken place in their lives.

Paquili led in his white Mercedes, pulling Ghuno's caravan, then Mochi in his Peugeot 404, also with a caravan in tow. I was third in the VW with Bianca, Mooka (another daughter of Paquili) and Clavel (Chiclo's sister-in-law) as passengers. Fourth was Narte, also a relative of Chiclo's, in another 404 with caravan and his wife Kali, and finally Chiclo himself, with his wife Dalila, bringing up the rear in their battered brown Simca estate.

The route varied little from year to year. Like other companies we stuck to invisible but established boundaries; all companies had their territories and were careful to avoid cramping each other's living space. It's a myth that Gypsies travel randomly and continuously; they have their set stopping places and invariably winter in one place, so while they are travellers they have also always been semi-sedentary wherever possible. Which is why we'd sometimes cover the 400 miles in two days, but more often in one long day to avoid stopping in places we didn't know.

Driving north, we soon stopped thinking of Mirabeau; being on the move was all that mattered. The children's eyes gleamed with excitement as we left behind the arid red landscape around Marseille, with its bare rocks and stunted trees, and turned into the Rhone valley, towards Valence, then cut across country and climbed upwards along tiny winding roads on the edge of the Massif Central, the air becoming thinner and fresh. We stopped for a brief lunch of salami, cheese, bread and wine; the views were breathtaking and the air so clean it was as if we could feel the last vestiges of Mirabeau's dust being swept away.

Mochi's car horn sounded more like a ship's foghorn and was especially loud. As we descended towards the lush lowlands north of Limoges he let rip, startling villagers who either laughed and waved or scowled and shook their fists, shouting, '*Vaches!*' (cows) or some other obscenity.

The last forty miles, nearly fourteen hours after leaving Mirabeau, we passed through fertile country with sheep and cattle grazing on lush green grass, cherry and chestnut trees, blackberries and apples and pears which would be ripe for picking before summer's end.

We were headed for Le Dorat, a small market town where we would always rendezvous with family not seen since the last *vendange*: the horse-drawn caravans of Ghuno's father, Zozo, and his cousin Nano. Le Dorat, with its *Poste Restante* office, was to be our contact base for the next couple of months.

It was late when we pulled onto the small patch of roadside turf set aside for nomads. As usual it looked as if the *gadjo* had searched long and hard to find the most uncomfortable site possible before designating it the official stopping place for nomads, but at least in Le Dorat they left us more or less in peace; they didn't insist on us moving on every two or three days, which was why it made a good base.

The fires were just smouldering embers and we could hardly make out the shadows of the two tall wooden caravans; everyone was asleep, but the dogs went wild, yapping and growling, and Paquili called out, '*Dobray tume Romale, sorve mishto?*' ('Greetings, *rom*, are you sleeping well?')

'*Cafe ya!*' Mochi demanded coffee.

Zozo's son Papi and Papi's cousin Jano appeared from underneath one of the caravans; they always slept outside, whatever the weather. When Papi stumbled over it wasn't coffee he offered but a litre of red wine, looking at us with his curiously different eyes, one ice-blue, the other almost black. 'You made it at last. Welcome, *pi pi*, drink drink, please.'

We wondered that the wine hadn't already been drunk; he must have been saving it especially, which was quite a gesture because Papi, hardly thirty, had had a serious drinking problem since his brief marriage ended in failure without children, and he wore an expression of permanent bewilderment, as if there were some fundamental point in life that he'd failed to understand. The family unit is the core of the Manouche world and a man without a woman is not thought to be really a man.

Jano slipped back into the shadows to confer quietly with Chiclo; he was a shy middle-aged man who was never very happy when there were too many people around. Then Zozo, who everyone referred to as *Cak*, 'Uncle', stepped down from his caravan and there were embraces all around. His wife Nana and the other women coaxed the fires back to life and soon the coffee was on the boil. We huddled around the low flames that would keep the Mulo, the death spirit that wanders the night, at bay and talked into the early hours, asking after everyone's health, hearing the news of winter, the same questions asked over and over again, the same stories told and retold until everyone was satisfied that they'd missed nothing. Everything was in order; the family was safe and together again.

In the morning we could see that the winter must have been harder for Papi than he'd admitted. His caravan was dirty and dilapidated, badly in need of repairs, but, worse than that, he'd had to sell his horse.

'The horse was old anyway,' he said, looking at the ground, shuffling ash with his boots.

'But an old horse is better than no horse,' Chiclo said. 'How are you going to move?'

Papi shrugged with resignation. 'I'll catch you up. I'll get another horse.'

Everyone knew that was probably not true, but there was nothing to be done and Papi didn't seek sympathy; it was what it was. We digested his information silently and turned our attention to something more immediate, such as what we were going to eat at midday.

Country campsite.

An Accident

L ife in the country was very different from Marseille. The men rose first, early, soon after dawn, all except for Paquili, who always lingered under the duvet for an extra couple of hours. The fires were stoked and water put to boil in a blackened pot while we ground the coffee beans by hand, then when it was ready we sat quietly sipping the thick sweet mixture from small bowls.

'We could go and look for some cane to cut,' Papi said, scratching his stubbled cheek and pouring his first glass of wine of the day. He offered the bottle around, but no one else was ready for wine that early.

'It's not the time for cane, it won't be ready yet,' Narte said without looking up. 'And the hedgehogs aren't fat enough yet. But we could go fishing at night.' Fishing during the day without permits was not really an option.

Plans were made, only to be forgotten again as the women started appearing and prepared the next round of coffee.

June and the beginning of July were especially quiet; it was too early for the fruit harvests or basket weaving, and the men had little to do apart from driving to shops and collecting wood, or bottles of water if the nearest fountain was not within walking distance. More often than not they sat about talking idly, sharpening knives and then blunting them again by whittling pieces of wood while waiting for the next meal-time. There was no rest for the women; they still cleaned and shopped and cooked and washed clothes, carefully hanging their undergarments out of sight of the men to avoid bad luck. The site itself was soon a bit of a mess, but the caravans were, as ever, spotless inside.

The men and women rarely ate together when there were several families travelling in a group. It was different from Marseille, where each family lived more or less as a separate unit. In the country, the men were served first, stew or soup, salami, cheese and bread, and ate with their knives, spearing pieces of meat and dipping lumps of bread in the stew. They passed around the wine, which was drunk straight from the bottle but without the bottle touching the lips, an art in itself, while the women and children sat a short distance away with their own food.

We smelled different in the country too, away from the grime of the city. It was an earthy mixture of woodsmoke, black tobacco and sweat, quite different from the *gadjo* with their pallid skin like Camembert cheese and their fainter and sweeter odour. If we were in a site close to a river and the weather was fine we'd often go for a swim, although not many men ventured into the water. They mostly preferred to wash from bowls of warm water while the women cleaned clothes by the riverside and waded in up to their waists fully dressed. We used sticks to pick our teeth clean; toothbrushes and toothpaste were rare. When I returned to London on one of my winter fundraising trips and visited a dentist again he told me my teeth were in perfect order, that cleaning them with sticks was almost as good as a toothbrush.

Going on an outing of any kind, to the shops or to pick up a spare part for a vehicle, was always a treat, something to lift the monotony of camp life, and whenever the car or van returned everyone else clustered around it. 'What have you got? Let me see.' Any news of any kind, however trivial, met an enthusiastic response from those with nothing better to do.

By mid-afternoon, some were starting to drink along with Papi (who was already half-cut), Jano quietly, and *Cak* happily. Sometimes the camp felt sad and isolated in those long afternoons, until the fires were lit and the evening meal beckoned.

If the weather stayed fine we'd lie up at Le Dorat for two or even three weeks, but it wasn't a comfortable site, bare of grass and with no rubbish bins. Anything that couldn't be burned was thrown in heaps outside and the place was soon dirty, while the nearest fresh water pump was a mile away. When it rained it turned into a muddy quagmire, and we moved.

Rubbish was a major source of conflict with the *gadjo*. The Manouche are judged by their rubbish-strewn sites and the grubby faces of their children, but no one seemed to have thought to maybe provide clean water or somewhere to put the rubbish for collection; it was easier to kick the can down the road to the next council. Within the caravans, the Manouche are probably even more hygiene-obsessed than the *gadjo* themselves, maybe out of necessity because of the conditions they live in. They'd never dream of washing clothes and cutlery in the same bowl, and any plate or glass carelessly left on the ground where a dog might touch it would be smashed and thrown away.

There were half a dozen villages dotted around the same region as Le Dorat which we visited in rotation. Oradour was a favourite; they'd really made an effort to provide at least some comfort instead of the obligatory minimal patch of wasteland for nomads. There was a small square field covered with thick grass and surrounded by high hedges, and in one corner even a water pump where everyone could enjoy makeshift showers and wash clothes without having to search for a river. The only problem was that we were never allowed to stay more than two or three days. As soon as we arrived the *klistey* would appear like magic to check everyone's papers, stamp them and then tell us how long we had. Maybe it wouldn't have mattered if everywhere provided similar facilities to Oradour's, but mostly it meant moving on to a roadside verge with no water, or a gravel pit, or even a rubbish dump.

The *klistey* rarely left us alone. In France, probably as in most European countries, nomads have few rights. There were frequent signs announcing *Nomads Forbidden to Stop Here*, and the Manouche carried special nomad papers, *Carnets de Circulation*, so they could be constantly monitored. We'd have our papers checked two or three times a week, my British passport causing some consternation.

'What are you doing here?' they asked every time.

'I'm living with them. I'm a journalist.'

A Gallic sneer, and my details were logged at the local town hall with the others.

A *carnet* one day out of date meant a fine, even if most couldn't read what was on their papers. Chiclo narrowly escaped prosecution for leaving his papers in the car while cutting hazel branches for cane a hundred yards away. The *klistey* tramped regularly through our camps, glaring around, making clear that we weren't wanted even if they had no choice.

There was sometimes more friction with the *gadjo* in the country too, maybe because our sudden appearance made us more obvious, intruders in an otherwise quiet and secluded world. Some were friendly and came with food, a chicken or sack of potatoes, to see if there was anything we needed and to satisfy their curiosity. But most viewed us with suspicion or outright hostility, shouting obscenities like 'Eat shit!' or 'Whores!' from the upstairs windows of their houses or bolting their doors as we walked through a village. If anything went missing within five miles of the camp, the finger of suspicion always pointed at us.

Roupenho went off on his own with his wife and children once for a couple of days, because they said they needed some time out together. He arrived back in a huge hurry in the middle of the night, something unheard of as Roupenho had a special fear of the Mulo. He'd been camped near a village and had bought a chicken, he had been seen carrying it back to his caravan, and the same day a farmer had said he had lost one of his hens. That evening a gang of farmers had accused Roupenho of stealing the chicken, shouting and rocking his caravan so that cups and saucers fell to the floor and smashed, terrifying his two small children. The *klistey* had arrived and Roupenho had shown them the receipt he had kept for his chicken, and he had been told to pack and leave to avoid further trouble. It's why you will rarely see a family of Manouche travelling alone; there's more safety in numbers.

The makeup of the company changed all the time on the road; almost every week someone would arrive to spend a few days with us, or some of us would go to visit another branch of the family elsewhere, occasionally travelling up to fifty or a hundred miles. I often joined an outing, enjoying the variety of scuttling back and forth between sites, until I lost my freedom of movement.

'The back wheels don't look right,' Mochi said one day, standing at the back of my VW, scratching at his crotch and under his armpits. 'The left one is at a funny angle.'

'And maybe you need a wash; you're scratching too much,' I replied.

Mochi gave one of his giggles; he rarely took insults to heart. 'Seriously, take a look.'

I took a good look underneath but couldn't see anything wrong, but then mechanics were never my strong point. Later I took Paquili and Nina a few miles to the nearest village to pick up some medicine for one of their children. On the way back, on a curve in the road, the wheel snapped off and we shot across the road towards a pile of logs. At the last minute I heaved on the steering wheel and the back of the van whipped around, sparks flying off the tarmac, and crashed into the log pile. We rebounded into the middle of the road, and the first thing I noticed, oddly, was that the radio had gone off, and then Paquili was hopping around clutching a knee and crying out in pain. Incredibly none of us had more than small cuts and bruises, even if Paquili's knee did swell up like a football and he was unable to walk without a crutch for a week or more.

The whole rear of the van was wrecked; only the front bench seat where we'd all been sitting was unscathed. All the inside fittings, the bed, the wardrobe, were in pieces. I sat by the roadside in shock and cried, my Gypsy adventure seemingly over again, while Nina and Paquili tried to comfort me as if I hadn't just nearly killed them. Luckily Mochi's 404 was the first car to appear after the accident, and with typical pragmatism it was decided there was nothing to do but strip the VW of anything of value, right down to the petrol, and sell what was left for scrap. It fetched ten pounds.

That night everyone in the company made a fuss of me while I still relived the accident and shuddered at the thought of what might have been. 'It's destiny,' tiny Ghuno said, passing me cup after cup of wine. 'It's a sign, you must accept it, so now you don't have your own van, but you don't have to leave. You can sleep under my caravan.'

Around midnight a tiny white butterfly hovered just above my head. 'You're going to get a message,' said Ghuno, staring at it.

'What do you mean? What kind of message?'

'I don't know,' she said, fixing me with her dark eyes. 'But it'll come tomorrow, that's what the butterfly is telling you, and it's usually good news.'

I was keeping only the most minimal of contact with the outside world, but she was right. The next day Chiclo drove me the twenty or so miles back to Le Dorat and there was a letter for me at the *Poste Restante* which had arrived that morning. It was from my sister Diane in the United States. She'd had a car accident; her Toyota had been wiped out by a Mercedes jumping some lights, but miraculously she'd walked away unhurt. Destiny. Ghuno. Butterflies at midnight. My mind was swirling.

Police harassment was constant; Narte and Paquili in the foreground.

Hedgehogs and Fish

After I lost the VW I slept wherever space was available. If the weather was fine, a sleeping bag under the stars was good enough, otherwise Mochi or Narte would let me sleep in their cars. I could no longer move around at will, but the upside was that for the short hops between sites, five or ten miles at a time usually, I climbed up beside Zozo, behind his horses, and entered a different world.

With two horses, Zozo could travel reasonably quickly if he wanted to, but he rarely did. A fifteen-mile trip would take a whole day, with a good long break for lunch, as we clopped gently along country lanes in the high caravan, which had been resealed with new plywood and painted blue and yellow. After fifty years roving the same small region, Zozo knew every little road and side road there was. Like most Manouche he couldn't read signposts but he didn't need to, and he always chose the quietest and prettiest routes with few cars, which was just as well because those we did encounter rarely slowed and often sounded horns to demand we move aside. The horses were unfazed; like their owners, they were used to harassment. We rolled gently along through manicured countryside, smoking hand-rolled cigarettes of black tobacco, picking out the different fruit trees, listening to the bees and the rhythm of the horses' hooves on the tarmac, and sipping from tumblers of rough red wine.

Apart from Zozo and his wife Nana, a wizened old lady who rarely spoke, and myself, there was also their daughter Lachi, a dark-haired and green-eyed woman, and her young son, and almost a whole farm-yard in the back of the caravan: chickens, a cock, a couple of dogs and a large black crow which liked to spend parts of the ride sitting on Zozo's cap, peering all around. Green-eyed Lachi and her illegitimate son were a problem in the company; she had brought dishonour to her family by sleeping with a married man, Tatey, and for two years the families had been avoiding each other. Tatey was still worried about the possible repercussions.

By midday it was time to search out a place to get the caravan off the road and let the horses graze while we had our lunch, but Zozo had all his regular spots. We would get a small fire going for coffee and lay out the bread, sausage and cheese that was our staple fare for much of the time. Zozo's pace of life was from another era again, in stark contrast to the motorised Manouche who raced about everywhere as if half the French army were after them.

'I've got my home right here with me,' Zozo said, throwing the dregs of his coffee onto the fire. 'So there's really nowhere for me to hurry to.'

The horse-drawn caravan also received a friendlier reception from the *gadjo*; they'd gather around and push handfuls of grass at the horses and peek inside the caravan.

'What do you do for a living?' a young woman asked once, shading her eyes from the sun with her hand.

'Steal children and sell them, of course,' Zozo said, to nervous titters. 'Or I could sell you a basket instead?' The old myth about Gypsies stealing children hadn't quite disappeared.

Summer wore on and the hedgehogs, the *nigli*, grew fatter, and we took to the fields with dogs.

'Give me a choice between a chicken and a fat *niglo* and I'll throw away the chicken every time,' Pantoon's father, Matzo, said once as we roasted several hedgehogs over a fire with lashings of salt and pepper. Other times we'd make ovens with bricks in the ground and cover and roast them that way. Bianca always wanted the feet, which became blackened and crunchy. Hedgehog was certainly a Manouche favourite, with a taste not far from pork but stronger and quite fatty. After a while I had to agree with Matzo.

The village of Adriers was one of our most fertile hunting grounds. Mostly we avoided sites which were too close to houses, but Adriers was the exception. The site was comfortable, more like an unkempt village green with plenty of long grass for the children to romp in, but it was completely encircled by houses and we always had an audience of *gadjo* watching from a safe distance. We'd have welcomed anyone who came into the camp and offered them coffee, but they never came close enough to talk; we remained outsiders.

As evening fell we looked carefully for the telltale trails which showed that the hedgehogs had started to move from their daytime hideouts, and as the dogs circled excitedly we dug and poked in thickets and hedgerows with wooden staves. Adriers was surrounded by fields, perfect *niglo* territory, and sometimes we took twenty or more in a night, but more often just a half-dozen.

Mostly it was only Chiclo, Narte, me and sometimes Matzo who went out; the others were too frightened of the Mulo, the *gadjo* without a head, as Adriers was generally accepted as one of his favourite haunts. The Manouche didn't fear much, but Beng, the devil, and his shapeshifting associates like the Mulo were an ever-present part of life.

In the evenings, sitting around the fire, we left spaces so that the Mulo could come and warm himself too and then leave without touching anyone. He represented death, and several of our company claimed to have seen him firsthand. He would suddenly appear by your side if you were walking at night in an unlit place and he could assume any shape, sometimes a woman with no head or a gigantic cat.

Narte swore he'd seen the Mulo disguised as a monstrous hedgehog, while another time Chiclo and Dalila parked their Simca on the road-side verge to sleep – I saw them park it – and when they awoke the car was out in the road; only the front wheels were still on the verge. They hadn't felt a thing, and everyone said that it was the Mulo.

Paradoxically the Mulo is attracted by fire, but it was also fire which gave us protection, which meant the flames needed to be kept down but the embers alight. If the flames were too big it was too much of an invitation, but if they went out altogether we were at the Mulo's mercy. Everyone became spooked if we were in a known Mulo site, and as night fell we'd huddle closer to the fire, the backs of our necks tingling, talking quietly until people drifted off in twos and threes, never alone. Even Papi and Jano sought inside space to sleep in those places.

With Chiclo I often walked up to five miles a night; even if we weren't catching much we enjoyed each other's company wandering the fields. When we were a long way from the camp and it was silent and dark, though, some of those tales of the Mulo went through our heads and we jumped at shadows in the trees and then turned back, tense. We would only relax when we heard the noisy confusion of the company, men and women shouting, dogs barking and children yelling.

One night a whole group stirred themselves to search for hedgehogs: Chiclo, Narte, Zozo, Mochi, Matzo, me and even Paquili, the only time I saw him make the effort. It was late in the evening but midsummer and still a dark blue twilight lingered, just enough for us to see each other and the two dogs criss-crossing the ground in front, trying to find a scent. We took a packet of hedgehogs that night, more than twenty, and the fields were freshly mown with a rich smell, and we picked wild cherries and nuts and wondered at the beauty of it all.

Mochi's shrill voice shattered the silence as we walked back to camp. 'It's twenty past ten.'

'You're wrong,' Paquili said. 'My watch says twenty-five past.'

'Bullshit, I set my watch by the radio this morning, I know it's right.' Mochi's voice went up a couple more semitones.

'Well, I set my watch by the radio too and I know I'm right.'

'Are you saying your watch is better than mine?'

And so they continued all the way back to camp. They loved an argument over nothing. When there wasn't a lot to do, an argument seemed to provide some meaning to everything.

Another afternoon Chiclo, Matzo, Mochi and I went out with the dogs and in the first field we saw maybe twenty cows and, in the middle of them, a big mean-looking bull.

'I bet we can run faster than some old bull,' Chiclo dared us.

'I bet we can,' I said.

'Not me,' said Matzo and Mochi simultaneously.

Chiclo grinned at me and we hoisted ourselves up to the top of the fence. There was a large chestnut tree in the middle of the field, about fifty yards away, but those cows were between us and the tree. We jumped together and ran straight at the cows, which scattered in panic. The bull was looking this way and that, trying to work out what was going on, as we made it to the tree and hid behind it, gasping for breath.

'Shouldn't have had that wine at lunch,' I wheezed as a round of applause went up.

We peeked around the tree to see the whole camp lined up, enjoying the show, which then of course just had to go on. We made several short dashes to the fence and back, going in opposite directions, and again the bull looked from one to the other of us, as if he couldn't decide which one to go after and was working it out. Eventually we decided it was time to leave before our luck ran out. By mistake we ran from behind the tree in the same direction and the bull came straight at us. We had a head start, maybe twenty-five yards, but I'm sure I could feel the ground shaking from the thunder of his hooves and could swear he was breathing down our necks. I reached the fence first and leapt over cleanly; Chiclo was just behind and scrambled over, ripping a gaping hole in his jeans as the bull juddered to a halt, glaring and snorting. There was a great whoop from the audience and everyone clapped, but we never tried an encore.

Fishing was less popular; only Narte really liked it. He even splashed out on a permit once, but Kali, his wife, ripped it up, saying he spent too much time by the riverside on his own, which had maybe been the point of the permit in the first place. Narte was a very dark man even by Manouche standards, small and compact, and carried no fat, just muscle. He looked most at home when out hunting or fishing, moving silently through the bushes, almost invisible. He spoke little and had an immense capacity for patient waiting; he could sit immobile for hours with a rod in his hands.

Once, when we were camped opposite some fields with a huge pond, I went with him. We slipped quietly out of the camp close to midnight; the moon was full and the land bathed in bright silver light, but the pond was surrounded by bushes which gave us plenty of cover. We'd had nothing but a watery soup to eat that day and we crouched by the water's edge, holding the lines that we hoped would provide food for the next day. Large water rats were gliding across the mirrored surface of the pond and we could hear the hollow *plop*s of fish rising, but the immense beauty of the scene was marred by a noisy village fête in full swing in a field on the other side. We listened to the laughter and music and imagined the tables laden with food and drink.

Narte suddenly jerked upright and pulled on his line with studied concentration, drawing it in hand over hand, until there was a thrashing in the water and he landed a good-sized perch.

'That's tomorrow's lunch sorted,' he said with a grin, his white teeth flashing briefly in his dark face. We stayed another hour or so and caught one more fish each before returning silently to camp, well pleased with the night's work.

Zozo with horses and caravan, near Le Dorat.

The author in Zozo's caravan; Lachi is standing behind.

The Mulo

By mid-July we began cutting hazel to dry into cane for weaving baskets, which the women would hawk around the villages, providing some extra income. The hazel branches were stripped of their bark and laid out to dry in the sun, and when they were ready the weaving was done by the men.

Narte, Jano and Papi were the busiest, each churning out several baskets a day, but Paquili was one of the most talented; he could make not just round but also perfectly oval baskets, with intricate patterns or the shapes of animals on the sides, although he rarely took the time to sit down and work. He'd been promising me a special basket for more than a year, but the closest he got was cutting the wood. When he arrived back with it, Nina started shouting at him because he'd been drinking too.

'Where do you find money for beer? We have nothing for food!'

Nina was a lazy woman but mischievous, and she needled Paquili constantly, except this time she'd picked the wrong moment. Paquili stared at her; they were standing close together and he towered over her, and then he hit her suddenly, lashing out, once, twice, not to the face but hard. She started screaming and there was pandemonium. Few doubted that Nina had provoked Paquili too far too often, but none of us had seen him strike out before. He grabbed the pile of newly cut hazel and threw it on the fire, where it smouldered and smoked, then he took his knife and cut himself twice on the arm, letting the blood drip to the earth before taking himself off to a corner to weep. No one liked seeing that.

Some days there really did seem to be an evil spirit about when everyone was getting into disputes, most often the hot listless days when there wasn't enough to do. The disputes rarely came to blows, but everyone started behaving like sulky children. Mochi accused Antoine, a mixed-blood married to a Manouche, Lamor, of stealing one of his cassettes.

'Paco de Lucia, I heard him playing it; it's my cassette!'

'I don't have your stupid cassette; I can afford my own,' Antoine, a lanky man with shoulder-length brown hair, shot back. He was a friend of Paquili's and was staying with our company for a couple of weeks. We never discovered the truth of the cassette, but Mochi and Antoine didn't speak again, or even eat together again; they just glared at each other, silently challenging each other, until one day Antoine had had enough and left.

Nearly all the families had their fallings-out; the only ones I never saw arguing were Chocote and Oumlo, and a sister of Narte, Volka, and her husband, another Matzo. Some of the women screamed and shouted and smashed crockery to vent their anger at their *rom*, usually over nothing very much, and the man in question would then refuse to eat, so other men would join him in sympathy and then no one got to eat; everyone would just sit around feeling angry with the world.

One of the few other times I saw someone actually strike out was when Papi was again off his head on wine. When he was drinking he had no idea what he was saying or doing; once he was so drunk he lay down for a snooze by the fire and rolled right into the flames, and by the time he woke up his leg was already badly burned. When he was sober he was the kindest, most helpful person you could imagine, but when he got drunk he wanted to fight the world. We ignored him, as no one wanted to take advantage of someone in that state, except on the afternoon when Papi lurched towards a fifteen-year-old.

'What you looking at? Do I know you? Anyway, I don't like the look of you,' he slurred, moving forwards aggressively.

The boy was a cousin of someone or other and just visiting for the day; he didn't know Papi and decided to get the first hit in, a perfectly timed blow which landed just above Papi's right eye and opened a large gash. Everyone rushed to hold the pair of them apart and the youth started to cry, but we were laughing; Papi had got his comeuppance. There was blood all over his face and he was jumping up and down.

'I just slipped; I'm ready. Come on, anyone,' he shouted, waving his fists around, but we just slapped him on the back and led him back to the fire to get his face seen to.

The bad days were always more than made up for by the good, especially as summer advanced and we became busier. Some days were just party days when we drove to a river to get the clothes washed. If there were any *gadjo* about they soon moved somewhere quieter; we were an unruly group, with tape recorders blaring from the vans, and the children screeching and running everywhere.

The washing done, Ghuno and the other women would lay out a feast of a picnic: cold meats and cheeses, olives, salad and baguettes and the obligatory litres of wine in plastic bottles. We'd spend the afternoon picking at the food, drinking, listening to anything from Travolta to Manolo, taking brief dips in the river and waving to passers-by because we were so happy and everybody else needed to be. By the time we stopped we were all tired, all except for Zozo; he'd dance forever as long as there was music and a glass of wine to hand. He would take his baby grandson in his arms and shuffle around the fire, his cap askew, a big smile on his face, and he just kept going until the baby was asleep. By then we were all ready to drop off to sleep as well, and we would go back to the camp and the caravans.

The children enjoyed incredible freedom, far more than their *gadjo* counterparts, brown naked bodies running and shouting all day, barely stopping to eat, and always looking for mischief. Most Manouche families were large; children represented security for the future and it was considered normal for a man to take a second wife if his first was barren. And the children could do no real wrong; if they did then it would be Beng who would be held accountable. Children were considered incapable of knowing guilt and so were ultimately blameless. Occasionally they attended school, but not often, and when they did they complained that they were picked on by the *gadjo* children and ignored by the teachers. In general the Manouche were keen for their children to learn to read and write, but beyond that schooling held little relevance for them and the lives they led.

'If we send our children away to become lawyers or doctors or some other profession, then they won't be Manouche any more,' Chocote said once as we sat by the fire discussing the merits of education, 'and that would be the end of us.' It was the same dilemma as the houses versus caravans; the Manouche were being squeezed on all sides.

Instead of going to school, the Manouche children learned early on to play an active role within the company. They grew up quickly and from ten or eleven years were expected to shoulder their share of the daily workload, especially the girls.

Bianca, at thirteen, was already like her mother; she never stopped working, and was always singing softly to herself. She was similar too in appearance to Ghuno, small and slim with large almond eyes that could stare at you with an intensity beyond her years and a long mane of thick black hair stretching down to her waist.

Apart from the cleaning and cooking, she also had to help look after a younger brother and baby sister who were both deaf mutes and mentally handicapped. Another sister, eleven-year-old La Muette, 'the mute', did her best to help, but hers too was a silent world and her efforts were limited. Bianca shouldered most of the burden; she never complained but seemed to pass from childhood to womanhood with barely time to catch breath in between. She became much more serious, and it was only when she was dancing one of her beautiful flamencos in the firelight that she looked like the child she really was again.

The boys had an easier time of it; they mostly led a life of leisure until their mid-teens, by when they'd be expected to do their part helping sort through the municipal rubbish tips and cutting grapes during the harvests, while keeping a beady eye open for any possible courtships. Only with marriage did a youth become a full-fledged *rom* and assume all the responsibilities and privileges that that brought, including being invited to eat with the other men.

Towards the end of July the days passed quickly, maybe because we knew some would be departing to visit family in Cognac, others towards Limoges to work the apple harvest, and still others back to Marseille to pick up those who'd stayed behind.

At one point we were camped a couple of miles outside the village of Verneuil-Moustiers, a place that the Mulo was known to frequent, and everyone was nervous.

'I'm going to bed,' Paquili said when it was not yet ten, standing up and beckoning Nina to follow him. 'This place gives me the creeps.'

Soon after, we heard the bolts on his van door being slammed shut. Mochi wasn't far behind; both of them had an especial dread of the Mulo.

That night, though, I felt I owed Mochi some payback, mostly for the fact he'd been the one to strip my wrecked VW without giving back anything; he was known to be exceptionally tight with his money. The night was inky and everyone had retired and shut themselves into their caravans and cars. I'd told Mochi's wife Sarah what to expect. Dalila lent me a blanket, and I waited with her and Lachi by the embers of the fire until everyone was well asleep; it must have been about two in the morning. I crept to Mochi's caravan and began scratching on the windows, prising one slightly open.

'The Saints save us!' Mochi yelped. 'There's something outside!'

'I can't hear anything,' Sarah said.

'There it is again. Maybe it's the dog?'

I yanked at the window again and tapped on the door.

'Have a look outside,' Mochi said.

'Not me; what if it's the Mulo?'

'I'm going to get my gun,' Mochi said.

I heard him heave himself from his bed and hid behind his car. By now the dogs had also set up an unholy din. The door to Mochi's caravan opened an inch, then a couple more; he popped his head out with the barrel of his shotgun, looked quickly around, then retreated and slammed it shut again.

The next morning he was white; he hadn't slept a wink and couldn't wait to tell everyone what had happened. No one let on; everyone agreed it must have been the Mulo. It was only when Mochi was fully packed, with his caravan hitched and ready to go, that we told him the truth.

'Bastards,' he said. 'Fucking bastards. But better that than it really was the Mulo!' And he unhitched his caravan again, shaking his head and muttering, smacking the bonnet of his 404 with his palm. It was one of the few times that he didn't really see the funny side of things.

Packing up and moving out at speed was an art the Manouche were well versed in, and they often needed to be, such as the time we were sharing a site with other companies. It was unusual, but as the harvests approached there were always space problems as the Gypsies stopped to wait wherever they could.

There were about thirty caravans bunched together, and adjacent to the site there were fields of ripening corn. The children lost no time in raiding the corn fields, bringing back sacks of cobs to roast on the fires, and the farmer went berserk when he saw the damage and called the police. Paquili banged on doors and just said, 'Move!'

There was no discussion; everyone knew their job as if it were an army drill, and within half an hour there wasn't a caravan left on the site. In that time we'd had to wake up children, take up bedrolls, dismantle gas stoves, take in clothes left to dry, grab chickens and any other junk and hitch up the caravans. Everyone left individually, as soon as they were ready. If the *klistey* did come, the fewer fines handed out, the better, and we always had prearranged places to regroup.

Bianca.

Papi basket weaving.

Zozo

Just before the end of July, when we were due to separate for a few weeks, Narte's younger sister Volka, a timid girl, small and dark like her brother with a mass of black curly hair, came and stood before me with her hands folded in front. She looked up through her fringe and asked if I would be godfather to her forthcoming child.

She was married to young Matzo, a roly-poly figure with a bushy black moustache, stocky and bearded. He was also reserved; they never raised voices at each other, but they were poor. They'd married young – she was not yet twenty and this was to be their third child – but Matzo still didn't have his own caravan; he was still waiting to take his driving licence, and so they slept wherever there was space on offer.

I was spellbound and readily agreed; Volka would become my *kirvi* and Matzo my *kirvo*, terms that replaced Christian names, I was becoming drawn ever inwards. She was still a good three months from birth, but they had asked me in advance, knowing that we would be splitting up for the *vendange* and reuniting in Marseille for winter when the baptism could take place.

*

Mochi had to make a couple of trips to Limoges in his 404 for the women to restock with goods for door-to-door selling, and it was always a good day out. Limoges was about forty or fifty miles from Le Dorat, and it was an astonishingly beautiful drive through lush green farmland bursting with produce, apples, pears, cherries, chestnuts, cows and sheep. It seemed like a place where nobody could ever go hungry. When we spotted other Manouche on the road we flashed our headlights and sometimes stopped to talk and drink green mint tea or red grenadine drinks at roadside cafés.

On the way back, if the roads were quiet, Mochi allowed his eldest son, six-year-old Siasco, to sit on his lap and take the wheel. Siasco was tiny even for his age, wiry and with a haystack of yellow hair that made his head look too big. I quietly fastened my seatbelt as he clutched the wheel while Mochi pushed down on the accelerator, laughing his high laugh, until we were hitting sixty miles an hour or more, but Siasco steered confidently and well, and we hurtled through the countryside without incident. In the back seat four-year-old Lele puffed on a cigarette; he was already developing a real fondness for tobacco.

'You shouldn't let Siasco do that, or at least not so fast,' I said. 'You could have got us all killed.'

Mochi gave another of his giggles. 'It's not a problem; I was watching him, and we are still alive, aren't we? That is all that matters.'

*

Even in the country no one apart from maybe Narte would leave the campsite on their own, whether to go to the toilet or just to wander through the fields, and again my habit of disappearing for walks at whim posed a problem. More than once I returned to the camp after a late amble under the stars to find that instead of everyone being asleep, half were waiting anxiously by the fire while others were out searching the fields and pathways with dogs. I had to promise never to go out alone again without first telling someone where I was going and for how long, and they watched the clock; if I was ten or fifteen minutes late another search party would be getting organised.

Television was rare when we were in the country; it was the guitar which dominated the evenings, the guitar and the big fire. Koki was one the best players, along with young Pantoon, who'd lost his virginity at Les Saintes. The two of them together would sit on logs and strum and tap their guitars in a fierce duel, and sometimes you'd see a *rom* holding the hand of his *romni* or with his arm about her. Public shows of affection weren't often seen, but these were romantic evenings, made for it, the yellow flames of the fire coming up from below so people's eyes were shrouded in shadow and mystery.

When most had gone to sleep, past midnight, Chiclo, Ghuno, Dalila and Lachi and I liked to stay on by the fire. Ghuno would stand and sing soft love songs, arms by her sides and head up, her thin crystal voice clear in the still night air, and it went right inside you.

We needed to return to Le Dorat to check for messages, but first, and before we split up for a few weeks, the dispute between Zozo and Tatey needed to be healed. Like Zozo, Tatey lived in a horse-drawn caravan. He was a thin man with a great drooping handlebar of a moustache, so you never knew when he was smiling or not, and his shoulders were always hunched. He was the father of Lachi's baby son, but he didn't want to take her as a second wife; he said he couldn't afford it.

Tatey and Zozo hadn't shared a campsite for two years; it was a bitter dispute but could have been worse. As it was, everyone was aware that Lachi had known that Tatey was already married when she had slept with him, so even though he had insulted Zozo she had to share the blame. If it had been otherwise, if she hadn't known that Tatey was already married and he'd tricked her, the blame would have been all his and would have created an irreparable rift, possibly even a blood feud. But Tatey knew he'd done wrong as well.

'He'll never forgive me,' he said, scuffing the dirt and playing with his moustache, his eyes darting around uneasily. 'He might even kill me.'

He was to become my second *kirvo* and it was disconcerting that he was the villain of the piece. He was usually the most inoffensive person imaginable, quiet and with a dry sense of humour.

Mochi and Paquili arranged the meeting between Tatey and Zozo, first going to Tatey's caravan at Le Dorat, a few miles away from where we were at the time, then returning to collect Zozo. I joined them in Mochi's 404 and we returned again to Le Dorat, where Zozo climbed out of the car.

'Come here,' he called gruffly to Tatey, pointing at the ground in front of his feet. Tatey looked apprehensively towards us before nodding quickly, then moved slowly towards Zozo, his head down.

The two men stood close together talking, Tatey always with his head down apart from an occasional quick glance up, Zozo gesticulating. Then they suddenly embraced and everyone heaved a huge sigh of relief; it seemed all was forgiven.

'I thought he was going to hit me at the very least,' Tatey said afterwards. 'And I deserved it.' And, if Zozo had hit him, Tatey wouldn't have been able to strike back; he was already in the wrong, and anyway hitting an elder like Zozo was unthinkable.

The next day, when we all moved back to Le Dorat, was a party day.

Return to Marseille

Mochi and Paquili headed off to Cognac at the beginning of August to visit relatives, while I drifted off to coastal resort towns to help Jean-Pierre sell T-shirts for a few weeks. It was his business at the time, photography in Paris not having really worked out, even if one day he was to become one of the leading television lighting experts in the city. He was tall and thin with very long legs, a short upper body and wide rounded shoulders, so when he stood thinking, as he often did, he looked like a back-to-front question mark. Despite the 'great strike' at his father's chateau we had remained good friends; he'd even visited London again in the winter and stayed with me at Eddy's house, where he was continually amazed by the sliced white bread that didn't go off within a few hours like a baguette, and he became a big fan of pool games and pubs. In the summers he'd taken to working the markets, from Royan on the Atlantic coast to Nice on the Mediterranean. He had a portable hot press and a choice of hundreds of stickers so punters could select their T-shirt design. It wasn't a great business – the hot pie and croissant stalls did much better – but it brought in just enough to keep me going until the *vendange*.

Zozo, Chiclo, Matzo and Narte meanwhile stayed behind, in or close to Le Dorat, until we regrouped. At least that was what usually happened, but in the year of the houses some of us needed to check on Chocote and Beudjeu and the others and see if they were still joining us for the *vendange*.

When Mochi and Paquili came back from Cognac, and I'd returned from selling T-shirts, we left for Marseille in Mochi's 404 one mid-morning, just the three of us, and drove hard, with few stops. Once, though, Mochi braked suddenly and came to a halt by an intersection.

'There used to be a big tree here; it's gone. Which way do we go?'

'Which way do you usually go?'

'Left of the tree, but it's gone!'

'Take the left-hand road anyway,' I said.

'How do you know?'

I pointed at the road sign which Mochi couldn't read. He grunted and put the Peugeot back into gear.

We also stopped to take fresh water at roadside fountains and for a snatched afternoon meal, and of course to have our papers checked. One *klistey* on a motorbike even did a U-turn as soon as he saw we were Manouche. The Manouche had recently become obliged to carry special markings on their number plates to make them easier to pick out and the police clearly took their duties seriously, but we were clean.

There was another small diversion when Mochi spotted three horse-drawn caravans camped in a valley.

'I think I know one of them, I'm sure I do,' he said, heading towards them.

He was mistaken, but there was an old white-haired *rom* there; he was blind in one eye and a young boy helped him to his feet.

'You look familiar to me,' he said, peering at Paquili with his one good eye.

An animated discussion followed, during which it turned out the old man had known Paquili's father some thirty years before.

'Give him my greetings,' he said, and Paquili nodded and said he would, without mentioning that his father now lived in a house.

We reached Marseille well after midnight, but Chocote was out of bed to offer food and coffee in his new front room even before the 404's engine had died. Lights went on in several other houses as the grapevine did its work and hours passed as we went from house to house, taking coffee, telling our news and listening to theirs, and feeling the strangeness of sitting at tables within cement walls. There were no fires outside; they'd been forbidden.

'You're living like peasants!' Paquili said.

'And you stink of hedgehog!' laughed Koki.

By the light of day we could see that Chocote had lost no time in making his patch the smartest in the street. There were forty houses in two rows, divided by a road. All the houses on one side were taken by Manouche, and all the ones on the other side were occupied by Jenische; they'd still kept their boundaries.

Chocote had a corner plot at the end of one row, so he had no neighbours on the side where he'd parked his caravan, which he still slept in. The house had lace curtains and a large television, pictures on the walls and a long sideboard showcasing Madonnas, china ornaments, cups and saucers, and copper and silverware. It gleamed; Oumlo scrubbed the floors three or four times a day, and outside Chocote had nailed a plaque to the wall, *Place du Niglo*. There was a bright green picket fence and gate at the front, the window shutters were blue and all the large stones around the flower beds had been painted bright red.

Next door, Paquili's father had been trying to copy everything that Chocote did, although he was discreet enough to use different colours. Other houses, like that of Zozo's brother Favo, were already falling into a state of disrepair. The front door was broken, the windows were without curtains, they'd made no compromises in lifestyle, and rubbish was strewn in front of the house, which was always full of people visiting, drinking coffee or wine, playing guitar or watching television. They treated the house as some sort of communal meeting room while continuing to live in their caravan.

Most of those who'd moved into the houses still had mixed feelings about them. Life was easier than in Mirabeau, where Beudjeu was still camped with his wife Pesi. There was running water and small kitchenettes, washing machines and indoor toilets, although the designers had installed sit-down toilets instead of squats, so most people took the seats off and squatted on the porcelain, or ignored the toilets altogether, sticking with the dockyards.

'It's healthier outside,' Blon said.

Overall the houses were seen as a good refuge, a place to rest up in comfort when not on the road, and they offered more security than Mirabeau. The Manouche were already semi-sedentary and the houses gave them a bolthole. Favo even got a job in the dockyards; every morning he marched off briskly at eight on the dot to do his eight hours in a warehouse. Food was more plentiful and regular than in the countryside.

A big downside was the gaggle of *gadjo* inspectors poking their noses into our lives, sociologists and even anthropologists. Never mind if we were in the middle of a meal; they'd barge in with their question sheets, making notes, nodding and tutting, like we were in a zoo.

While Chocote and Oumlo continued to sleep in their caravan, I slept upstairs on the house mezzanine with Blon and his two youngest brothers, Niglo and Pepite. It was unbelievably hot, thirty-five or forty degrees Celsius, made worse because there were no trees offering shade and the houses created a heat trap. Chocote was incredibly house-proud; he even pottered about from time to time with a duster in his hand, and he built a dry well in his front yard by sinking a large piece of hollow concrete into the ground. Oumlo used it for flower displays.

Oumlo loved her flowers; she collected cuttings everywhere. It was probably the only thing she really liked about being in a house. Otherwise she looked tired and drawn.

'We eat, we clean, we sleep, we get up and we eat again, over and over again,' she said sadly as she swept the floor for the umpteenth time. 'I miss the country. I can't wait for the *vendange*, to live like a Manouche again.'

'You're definitely coming, then?'

'We'll be there; I wouldn't miss it. Otherwise, what, we just sit here in the sun and bake? The *vendange* is like a holiday for me. Chocote knows that,' she said, finally putting aside her broom.

The tendency towards crime had become more noticeable amongst the youths since the move into the houses. It was no longer pilfering food or stealing cars for joyrides before dumping them. It was as if the younger Gypsies felt that if they had to live in houses, then they wanted a share of what they thought that lifestyle should be. There were rumours of house break-ins and even drugs, and there were fights with Arab gangs in the city. The police raided some of the Jenische houses one day; a whole wagon of them arrived with automatic carbines and riot gear, and they dragged off four young men, savagely kicking one who was a bit slow. I grabbed my camera and started taking pictures as a social worker started shouting at the police.

'Stop that, you can't hit people like that!' she yelled.

The *klistey* ignored her and then one spotted me and ran over, snatching the camera and taking out the film before checking my papers. We never found out what the Jenische were supposed to have done.

Paquili and Mochi returned to Limoges to prepare to move their caravans down towards the Gironde, while I stayed on in Marseille for another week. We tended to sleep longer in the houses; there wasn't much to get up for except to go with Beudjeu to a rubbish tip a couple of times. The rest of the day we played endless games of *boules*, or lay on the cool floor tiles of the house in the heat of the afternoon, watching television. The favourite shows were Westerns or kung-fu movies, or series like *The Saint* or *The Six Million Dollar Man*. Another big hit was *Rich Man, Poor Man*, and once we saw our own company on the screen; it was an old programme on the Manouche being given a repeat outing. There was a much younger Paquili, and Bianca when she was six or seven years old. The interviewer asked her if she liked to speak French.

'No, I like to speak Manouche.' She looked straight at the camera, her big eyes deadly earnest.

'And what about school? What have you learned there?'

'They taught me to read; I can read *Mama* and *Papa*.' And then Bianca ran off out of shot, while Paquili beamed proudly.

The television was left on all day and it was a problem. Already French was heard more and more; the Manouche culture was being stifled.

'The children will have a hard time of it,' Chocote said, sitting in the shade at the front of his house. 'They are no longer travellers in the old way, they are forgetting their language, but in the city they are at the bottom of the pile, they're not free.'

Beudjeu ran a hand through his black hair and spat. 'They put us in houses and force us to learn their ways in schools, but then they don't accept us,' he muttered angrily.

He had a point. No effort was being made to preserve the Manouche culture and language. On the contrary, all the pressure was for the Manouche to forget their old habits and become more French, to take their place as settled albeit underprivileged members of society. Even the guitar was heard less and less.

Pantoon with the new houses behind, Marseille docks 1980.

The Gironde

Paquili and Mochi came back briefly to collect social security payments, and they told us they'd moved their caravans to a camp-site at Les Billaux, not far from Libourne, in the Gironde. They urged us to join them.

'You should see it; there must be fifty caravans together!' Paquili said excitedly.

'So many fires at night,' squeaked Mochi.

Maybe it was all the talk of the country and the fires and the Manouche gathering, but that night there was a festive mood. We even risked a fire in a brazier, and we drank and sang and listened to duelling guitars until well after midnight, Chocote and Koki, Pantoon and two of Chocote's nephews, Julian and Luis, and it was like the old times again.

The next afternoon there was an urgent phone call for Paquili. It was Nina, and she said the police had been to the site and told everyone to leave; the local council had decided there were too many Manouche together at Les Billaux after residents had complained about the mess. Now there were just the caravans of Paquili and Mochi left; no one had a driving licence to move them off the site, and they had no money left for food. Nina also said they hadn't eaten for two days, which was prob-ably an exaggeration even if they'd only had soup.

Paquili and Mochi left within the hour, and Matzo senior, Pantoon's father, said he'd join them with Koki and me a couple of days later.

It was still night when we left, about four o'clock, because Koki's papers weren't in order and we wanted to slip out of the city without trouble, two blue Saviems hastily fitted with beds and gas cookers. Matzo led with me, his wife Nanine, a very pregnant Catalonian, and their six children: Pantoon, his younger brother Lalu (who devoted all his waking hours to looking for trouble, usually quite successfully), and their four sisters, Mooka (meaning 'little fly'), Lacloc (whose speciality was biting people), Linda, and baby La Poule.

The journey was an ordeal; instead of the usual twelve hours it took double that. Koki's van lost a set of brake pads after barely a hundred miles and it took hours to find a car dealer with the parts we needed. Once the new brake pads were fitted, we skirted Carcassonne with the rugged beauty of the Pyrenees on our left, then threaded through the industrial wasteland of Toulouse and on, following the setting sun westwards into the night. Matzo kept himself awake by rubbing a damp cloth over his face and chain smoking, until at last we pulled into Les Billaux with the sky already lightening again, except now the sun was coming back up behind us.

Most of the area had been fenced off even though it was the only site for miles around at the busiest time for travellers. A small muddy space of about fifteen square yards had been left. Apart from the two caravans belonging to Paquili and Mochi, there were a few others from our company including Passete, a brother of Chocote, and Roupenho, who also had young Matzo and Volka in the back of his van. Everyone was still asleep, but the sound of our engines woke them up. Gas lights appeared in the windows, and then Ghuno emerged to dig in the ashes of the fire, blowing on the embers until there were flames and putting on a pot of water to boil. Soon we were all standing around a magnificent blaze, watching the feeble rays of the sun spreading across the sky and clutching steaming mugs of coffee.

Volka approached with a tiny bundle, smiling shyly. '*Kirvo*,' she said, 'here is your godson.'

He was a big baby, just two days old, with thick black hair already, and his birth certificate named him *Nadjo*, which was as close as the Manouche could get to my name. I hugged Volka and shook Matzo warmly by the hand, overcome with emotion, and we agreed to hold the baptism after the *vendange*.

'I'm so happy,' I told them. 'I feel very proud to be your *kirvo*.'

Passete's caravan was a welcome sight; we didn't see him every year, but when we did there was never a dull moment. He had eight sons plus this time a cousin, Bidoo, who'd left his own parents and siblings to move in with Passete when his immediate family had opted to live in an apartment in Bordeaux.

'I belong on the road, not in some stinking apartment,' Bidoo said, looking at himself in the mirror and combing his blond hair. Apart from being fair and very vain, he was also tall and thin, and everyone poked fun at him, saying he had the *English fever*.

Ten men and one woman meant it was impossible for poor Vita, Passete's wife, to cope alone, and it was the only time that I saw Manouche males helping out with washing the dishes and cleaning the caravan and car. They drew the line at laundry.

I started spending a lot of time with Bidoo and Nanoon. Away from the camp, they could easily be mistaken for *gadjo*; they were quite particular about their clothes and appearance, and Nanoon didn't even have a moustache. He was the elder of Passete's two still unmarried sons; the other was Topo.

Being back in the country felt wonderful and we forgot about the problems with the site for a few days, relaxing back into the rhythm of the outdoors. Roupenho, looking several pounds heavier, drove the women into Libourne the first morning. They came back with mounds of raw salted sardines and mackerel, salad, bread and wine, and we sat to eat and drink and soak up the warmth of both the people and the sun.

The Gironde is almost nothing but vineyards; after a while it becomes quite dull scenically. There are no cows or sheep and few trees, just rows and rows of vines marching away into the distance, and it's poor land for hunting, whether it's game fowl or hedgehogs you are after. Maybe it's the pesticides they use on the vines, or maybe it's that the Gironde is one of the most heavily hunted regions in a hunt-crazy country. Every evening and especially at weekends the French were out shooting at anything that moved. Once someone loosed off a couple of barrels from a shotgun into the side of Chiclo's parked Simca for no apparent reason, even if it was so battered anyway the pellet marks made little overall difference. When we went out at night to look for hedgehogs we wore dark clothing and moved cautiously.

Hedgehogs were scarce, but there was no end of fruit and nuts, especially blackberries, which we'd spend hours collecting. We'd mash them up with sugar and gorge ourselves until our mouths were stained black and our stomachs swollen.

There was a small stream running by the site at Les Billaux, and when it rained on the third day we saw why the place was so muddy. The stream quickly flooded and soon we were wading about, anxiously watching the water as it rose up the wheels of the caravans. It was too late to get out of the site, the road was already under several feet of water, and life became miserable; we were wet all of the time.

It was made worse because the stream flowed from the Dordogne river, which is tidal, and there was a full moon, which meant the water level was rising more than usual. Three times we watched the water rise until it was lapping at the doors of the caravans and three times we watched it recede again. We didn't want to move because there were no other official stopping sites nearby.

Nanoon took a soaking when one of Passete's dogs, a big black mutt, got another by the throat and wouldn't let go. Nanoon threw them into the stream, and when they still didn't part he jumped in after them. We watched as they thrashed about, before Nanoon took a log and whacked the mutt about the head until it was nearly unconscious and slowly loosed its grip on the other dog.

Midway through the second day of flooding we called it a day and started to pack up. Roupenho went first, then after a moment's hesitation Paquili followed, and Matzo and Koki too. We were soon strung out along narrow grass verges by the road. It was a bad place to be; all the time we had to watch the children because of the danger of passing cars, and we knew the police would be along sooner or later to move us on, but Les Billaux was fast becoming uninhabitable. It was another example of how local authorities seemed to go out of their way to find the worst place possible for the Manouche to stop. Leeches were washed in on the tidal flow and the dogs started getting mange, and everyone was beginning to get rashes. We were itching all over.

The first time the *klistey* came, nobody made a fuss and we returned to the official site, but hours later we were back on the roadside as the water began to rise again.

The next time we moved without warning. At the time I was out with Nanoon looking for somewhere to work the *vendange*, because we'd found out that Jean-Pierre's father had decided to use machines instead of people for that year's harvest, so we were redundant. Finding a new place was proving difficult.

'He could have told us before,' Paquili had grumbled when we'd heard, throwing a log onto the fire and lighting a cigarette. 'He's got Meme's number in Marseille. And we've worked for him for years.'

Machines were taking over everywhere; it was the same with the apple harvests further north. In any case, when Nanoon and I got back to our roadside spot there wasn't a caravan in sight. We drove on to Les Billaux, but that was deserted too, except for one very poor family with a battered horse-drawn caravan, and they didn't know anything, just that the *klistey* had been there moving people on, so we waited.

Soon Chiclo came back to find us and we followed him to our new site, a gravel patch under a dual carriageway flyover. We stayed there for several days. Every time a Manouche caravan passed overhead it sounded its horn and we waved back, but we weren't comfortable there; we had to go miles to fetch fresh water and it was noisy, with no privacy.

We eventually moved to a beautiful riverside plot that Tatey and Django, an old friend of Chocote's, had found. It was near a village called Abzac, about ten miles from Libourne, and right on the banks of the Dordogne, surrounded by maize fields. There were signs everywhere saying *Forbidden to Nomads*, but we were beyond caring by then.

Money was short; not having a place to work was a shock. We'd driven 400 miles from Marseilles for the harvest and now we were at a loss. The women had to go out hawking all day every day, walking for miles, knocking on doors to earn whatever they could, usually three or four pounds for food. Chiclo and I poached a small duck from one of the farms, but decided to keep it and fatten it up until it was worth eating, which was a mistake. When we left the camp one time young Lalu took it upon himself to kill the bird, pluck it and gut it and cook it over the fire, and by the time we returned he'd scoffed the lot.

The local thieves were working overtime as well, judging by the number of visits we had from the *klistey* and the constant searches. With the large number of Gypsies in the area it was obvious where the suspicion would fall, and some felt, if we were going to get the blame anyway, we might as well make it worthwhile.

Topo said he knew of one band of Manouche nearby who had taken to breaking into shops at night to take whatever they could, cameras, watches and food, but that didn't happen within our group. We felt that if you were going to be suspect number one from the outset, then what was already a risky business became near suicidal. Our main ambition was to keep a low profile and not get noticed by the police; the Manouche had a special dread of incarceration. About the worst that members of our company got up to was siphoning diesel or petrol from unattended cars in the back streets of Libourne; fuel was a valuable commodity for the Manouche. But there was one youth who used to visit us sometimes: his name was Murga, which meant 'cat', he was married to the sister of someone from our group, and he went much further.

When we were walking down the street of a small village, a *gadjo* left his expensive Citroën DS with the engine running as he quickly went into a shop for cigarettes, and without a word Murga was into the driver's seat and away before I knew what was happening. The expression on the owner's face when he came out was hilarious; he could still see his car disappearing down the road, and he spluttered and shouted impotently, shaking his fist. By the time he'd got hold of the police his precious car was well on its way to a Bordeaux breaker's yard.

I saw Murga again that night and he was in high spirits.

'Don't tell anyone,' he said. He was a wiry man with shoulder-length black hair and a small scar on his left cheek. 'I got 5,000 francs for it,' which probably meant he'd got at least double. He offered me a hundred, but I politely turned him down and assured him his secret was safe.

'The best night I ever had was when I broke into a priest's house.' He grinned mischievously.

'A priest's house? Around here?'

'No, it was south of Bordeaux, I don't remember the name of the place. I got in through a window that he'd left open and looked everywhere for his money – priests always have money – but I couldn't find a thing, and all the time I could hear the guy upstairs snoring his head off. Maybe he was drunk, but it sounded like a chainsaw.'

'So what happened?'

Murga leaned forwards conspiratorially. 'I realised the money must be in his room, so I went up there and carried on searching, and then I stood there listening to his racket and thinking, and then it hit me: the loot had to be under his pillow!'

'Don't tell me . . .'

'Yes. I crept to his bedside and was just getting my hand under the pillow when he gave a great snort and turned over; I nearly died of fright! But he didn't wake up, so I put my hand under again and felt his wallet. I pulled it out real gently and opened it for a quick peek and saw a big wedge of cash, then quietly left the way I'd come.'

'How much did you find, then?'

'More than 7,000 francs, can you believe that? What does a priest need with all that cash?'

'What did you do with it?'

'Had a big party, of course!' Murga laughed out loud and a few *rom* by the fire turned to see what the joke was.

A Marriage

Chocote joined us early in September. 'I had to practically drag him away from the house,' Oumlo said, standing by the fire and sipping coffee, her eyes twinkling with amusement. 'I don't think he really wanted to come, but I wouldn't take no for an answer.'

Niglo and Pepite were with them in their Saviem; Chocote hadn't gone so far as to uproot his caravan from its new permanent mooring spot in Marseille. There was also Beudjeu, his wife Pesi, Blon and Gege, one of Favo's sons, in a Peugeot van: blue, of course.

Chocote was quick to notice the forest of signs forbidding nomads where we'd camped. It was a perfect spot with the river and shade and cornfields, and so far the police had left us alone, maybe because we'd been very careful about keeping the site clean, but Chocote was adamant: we had to move back to Les Billaux. His big mantra was to avoid conflict with the *klistey* at all costs, and if that meant crowding into a muddy field, then so be it.

We were now close to a dozen cars, vans and caravans, a big group for the continual disruption of moving. And when we arrived at Les Billaux we found a scene of complete confusion; there were at least thirty other families waiting in front of us, hundreds of people squeezed onto the side of the road, arguments and shouting up and down the line. The site itself was full, and a couple of caravans had just stopped in the middle of the road, blocking it. The police arrived quickly in two cars and told everyone to leave.

'Where to?' I asked a smooth, immaculately dressed young officer in dark sunglasses, and he smiled.

'My job is to move you, not tell you where to go.'

'But there *is* nowhere to go. This is the only official site for miles, and it's full.'

'I'll be back in two hours; if you're still here I'll have every one of you prosecuted.' And he left us, blue lights flashing.

Chocote and Passete drove halfway to Bordeaux to check out the only other official site they knew, but it too was overflowing, so we ended up under the flyover again: all except Django and Tatey, who said the site at Abzac by the river was worth the risk. They were right, and with another week or two to wait until the *vendange*, assuming we found work, everyone else followed them. Even Chocote was prepared to risk a fine rather than stay under that bridge.

The police did come, but after a lot of gesticulating and threats they saw reason; they could see we were looking after the site and decided to give us a chance. They wrote down all the registration numbers of our motley array of vehicles and said we could stay on the site until the *vendange*, and that we'd only be prosecuted if we left the place in a mess.

Chiclo and Zozo also arrived, and there were two other horse-drawn caravans down from Cognac alongside us. One was really special; it had a long wheel base and weighed two tons unladen, and inside it was all wood-panelled, with a raised bed at the back hung with lace.

Abzac was the perfect campsite: there were plenty of trees and grass, we had the river where we could fish and swim and wash clothes, and the children were free to run and play as we passed some exquisitely lazy days.

With hundreds if not thousands of Manouche camped all over the region waiting for work, it was also a busy time for romance. The young men spent an inordinate amount of time cruising in their cars, visiting other groups of friends or relatives, ostensibly just socially but with a hungry eye open for any possible match. A Manouche marriage doesn't involve a church ceremony, or any other kind of ceremony. Sometimes it's an arrangement between parents, but more often it's two people deciding they want to live together and eloping. If you can get through the first night together without an angry parent arriving on the scene, then you are considered married. Most young couples stayed away for several days, enjoying a sort of mini-honeymoon, before returning to their families, where they'd be fêted.

Bidoo took us all by surprise when he decided to get married. We were on a night out to Bordeaux in Nanoon's Peugeot 504. First we picked up Nanoon's girlfriend, a *gadje* called Francoise, and then Bidoo said he wanted to visit his fiancée at Potop's camp.

'Fiancée?' I asked. 'Since when were you engaged?'

'Since now. Well, a few days ago,' Bidoo said sheepishly.

'Seriously?'

'Yes, seriously. Can we just go?'

Nanoon and I looked at each other and shrugged, smiling.

Potop's site was just on the outskirts of town, and we drove in and stood by the fire and exchanged greetings. Potop was a distant cousin of Passete; he was a big man with the customary drooping moustache worn by so many of the Manouche, and known to have an evil temper.

The visit dragged on while Nanoon disappeared with Francoise somewhere for a cuddle. Potop's older daughter, another Nanine and still a teenager, a pretty girl with shoulder-length black hair and glittering dark eyes, kept shooting glances at Bidoo, who looked back dreamily; it was hard not to notice.

Some who'd been out hunting returned with a couple of rabbits. The fire was getting low and people were drifting off to bed, and still we stayed. Shortly before midnight, Potop scratched his head and looked at us curiously, then bade us goodnight.

As soon as Potop had disappeared into his caravan, Nanoon appeared at my side. 'Get in the car, quick!'

I clambered into the front passenger seat and Bidoo and Nanine hurried into the back, holding hands.

'If you don't take me tonight I never want to see you again,' she whispered.

Bidoo fell for it. 'Yes, I'm ready, let's go, quickly!'

'Are you sure about this?' Nanoon asked Bidoo. Everyone was whispering because we were still in the camp and at any moment Potop might come out looking for his daughter. 'You're only twenty, you've got your whole life ahead of you, and where will you live?'

'Just go!' Bidoo hissed. 'Get the hell out of here!'

We moved slowly through the camp without lights, the atmosphere inside the car charged with emotions, love and anxiety and passion and nerves, until we hit the road and Nanoon slammed his foot down on the accelerator. 'So where are we going? Did you think about that, at least?'

'Take us to the train station,' Bidoo said. 'I've got family in Pau and we can stay with them.' Pau was a good way south, in the foothills of the Pyrenees.

Then Bidoo beat his fist against his forehead. 'Oh, dear mother, what have I done? What have I done?' But he was smiling, and so was Nanine in quiet excitement.

Nanoon and I continued to study the lights of the cars behind, making sure none belonged to Potop giving chase. Sometimes if a father is against a marriage he will go after the eloping couple and try to take back his daughter by force, but he's got to do it before they spend the first night together. After that it's too late; the marriage is consummated.

We reached the station in record time and hurried into the booking office, which was of course closed by then; the last train to Pau had left hours ago, and there wouldn't be another one until the morning. Bidoo buried his face in his hands; he was nervous and it showed.

'Good thinking,' Nanoon said. 'Don't suppose you checked the timetable.'

'Shut up!' Bidoo told him. 'You're not helping. What do I do?'

'Go to a hotel?' Nanoon suggested.

'No, it's too risky. Take me to my sister's instead,' Bidoo decided. 'She's not far away.'

He gave us directions to the site, which luckily was nearly empty.

We woke Bidoo's sister and told her what had happened. She became emotional and hugged Bidoo and began making up a bed for them. '*Zinder, zinder,*' she said: 'poor dears, poor dears'. 'Don't you worry, you'll be fine here, and if that Potop dares to show up I'll make such a fuss that you two can escape through the back window.'

Bidoo didn't want to be left alone straight away, so Nanoon and I stayed on another hour or more, until about two in the morning, but there was no sign of a pursuit and we finally drove back to Abzac. When we told Nanoon's mother Vita the next morning she cried for hours, but they were tears of happiness. Potop, of course, had guessed what was going on and had accepted it, so there had been no pursuit anyway.

Divisions

Nanoon and his brothers were keen boxers; they had proper gloves and head protectors and every evening they'd spend an hour or so hammering away at each other, until the sport caught on in the whole camp. Chocote bought more gloves for Niglo and Pepite and we arranged boxing tournaments by age group. Mostly we tried not to do each other any damage, avoiding face shots and going for the side of the head, but sometimes things got heated if a boxer felt that honour was at stake and the match would be stopped. The funniest were the children, four-year-olds wearing gigantic boxing gloves and swinging punches with all their might until one inevitably lost his balance and ended up on his backside. I wasn't very good at it. I thought I was quite good at most sports, but boxing was something different; a five-minute round was more exhausting than any football or rugby game I'd played in, and usually I got a good hiding.

We started looking for work with more determination, driving to different properties at random. It was difficult finding a place for such a large group with a new patron who didn't know us; it wasn't as if we were carrying references. Some didn't even open their doors, and one simply threw open an upstairs window and shouted, 'Go away, we don't need anyone!' But towards the end of the third day, near the village of Fronsac, we struck gold, calling on a chateau with a young manager who was looking for *vendangeurs* who needed neither food nor lodgings. My presence intrigued him and seemed to tip the balance.

'You're English?' he asked, his hands in the pockets of his smart-casual trousers. He had black hair swept straight back from his forehead and a sharp nose, and like many people in the Bordeaux region he was a confirmed Anglophile. 'I lived for a year there before coming here; I worked on a vineyard in Hampshire. The white wine

was quite good; not like French wine, of course, but not bad ei
What are you doing with these people?'

I gave him my usual story about doing a documentary – it was eas
than giving him my confused life story – and said I'd known o
company for several years. 'They're good people; they won't give yo
any trouble,' I said.

We tried to haggle over how much we'd be paid, but he wasn't having
any of it and told us we'd have to accept the rate set by the regional
wine producers' syndicate or nothing at all. Still, he was very straight-
forward and spoke to us like equals, which impressed Chocote; the
Manouche weren't used to that.

'But the harvest won't start until the very end of September or
maybe even October,' this new patron, Monsieur Bigaud, said. 'The
grapes are still too dry; we need some rain.' It was his first harvest in
charge at the chateau; he'd been hired by the owner at the beginning of
the year and he needed to make a success of it. After we'd agreed
terms, he showed us a large grassy piece of land to one side of the
chateau where we could camp until the harvest started.

Chocote was delighted, he had his security, but Paquili scowled.

'It's not worth it for me; I've only got Ghuno and Bianca to help me
in the vineyards,' Paquili said. Nina was confined to camp with her
youngest child and wasn't able to work. 'There's no money in it for me;
it's too long to wait. I'll be better going back to Mirabeau.'

Roupenho went with him; he needed to get his nomad papers
stamped, something which had to be done every year, and that meant
Matzo and Volka had to leave as well because they'd nowhere to sleep
except the floor of Roupenho's van. I said I'd see them in Marseille for
Nadjo's baptism after the *vendange*. At the last minute Koki also decided
to join the exodus after a furious row with his wife Tac-Tac, who
wanted to stay.

'We have no money,' Koki said, kicking at the tyres of his van. 'We
can't last until the *vendange* starts, even.'

'We can borrow some, or sell baskets, or hunt,' Tac-Tac countered,
arms crossed and pouting.

'We are completely broke, don't you understand? We probably don't even have enough diesel to get back to Marseille; we'll need to find some.'

'And what will you do in Marseille? Steal?'

'Of course not, I don't steal, but I can get some social security at least so we can eat.'

'We can eat here; the others won't let us starve.'

And so it went on, but Koki felt his honour didn't allow him to live off the charity of others and he insisted on going, which was a shame because he was one of our best guitar players.

Before they all left we had cause for one more big party. Passete and Vita hadn't spoken to each other for three months after some domestic row or other; apparently it had started because Passete had lost his temper and used extremely harsh language when angry with one of his sons, which Vita didn't accept. All that time they'd continued living together, she carrying out her family duties, he doing his, and speaking to each other only through Nanoon or one of his brothers.

It fell to Chocote in his role of mediator and peacemaker to bring them together and start them talking to each other again, which he somehow managed after nearly an hour in their caravan. No one knew what was said, but the three of them eventually emerged with broad smiles, and Passete held Vita's hand and told her she was the finest woman any man could have.

The camp went wild. Passete brought crates of beer and at least twenty litres of wine, and even Chocote, who rarely drank alcohol, got stuck in. Koki sang in Spanish, with Pantoon and Niglo taking turns to accompany him, and everyone was dancing, even Oumlo, who rarely danced in case Chocote disapproved of her showing her feelings in public. Not for the first time, it was Chocote who brought the evening to a close as he took the guitar and sang beautiful laments about the Manouche, songs of bitter loneliness and rich friendships. Tears streamed down his weathered face, and when he finished no one made a sound, not even the children; there was just the crackling of the fire and it was as if we were bound by a spell.

After Paquili and the others had left, we idled the days away waiting for the *vendange*. We didn't often bother with searching for hedgehogs; they weren't plentiful amongst the vineyards and it was cold work at night at that time of year.

Pantoon's father, the elder Matzo, took me on a disastrous foray one evening. We were following his two dogs, waiting for the yapping that would tell us something had been found, and when it came we ran forwards to snatch up the *niglo* quickly before the dogs could turn it over and start eating it themselves. It was important to grab the hedgehog and turn away in one fast movement to stop the dogs jumping up at it, but this time I turned too slowly and one of the dogs took a chunk out of my finger.

'Shit, that hurt!' I sucked on my finger, holding on to the hedgehog.

'Show me,' Matzo said. He tutted. 'It's not too deep; it should heal.'

On the way back, Matzo walked into a barbed wire fence in the dark, ripping his jacket almost in half as he pulled free. And all we had were three hedgehogs.

Maybe it was lack of care or river swimming that did it, but three days later my finger had swollen to the size of a small cucumber, there were red traces reaching up to my elbow, and I was running a fever and getting dizzy spells. Being ill like that while living on the floor of a caravan was miserable. By the fire on the afternoon of that third day, Chocote, on his customary seat under an umbrella while everyone else stood, pointed at his heart.

'If that red keeps going to your heart, it's the end,' he said sombrely. 'It's infected. You must find a doctor.'

Chiclo drove me straight into Fronsac to find a doctor. I had no money left and had to call Jean-Pierre to ask him to come. He was at his father's property in Saint-André-de-Cubzac, which wasn't far, and, good friend that he was, he arrived within the hour. The doctor, a chubby and fussy man wearing a *pince-nez*, reassured that he would be paid, gave me four injections and antibiotics for two weeks.

'Make sure you wash the wound properly, at least twice a day,' he said.

Ghuno put aside a drinking bowl, which I used for cleaning the wound. When the infection finally disappeared and I'd finished with it, she smashed the bowl.

Narte with catapult.

The Preacher

It was Chiclo who took me to a strange religious ceremony one day. The Manouche were Catholics in theory but not in practice, and there was a growing evangelist movement within their ranks, a curious blend of Christian teaching and traditional Manouche spirit worship and belief in the supernatural.

'It's the second time I've come, but I don't really believe in it,' Chiclo said as we arrived at a small red brick hall deep in the countryside.

Inside we found we weren't the only inquisitive ones from our company. Standing at the back of the hall were the older Matzo, Tatey and Django, along with about fifty other Manouche. A guitar struck up and there were a few songs, before the preacher or priest, or whatever he was, called upon his audience to speak out about miracles they had witnessed. He was also a Manouche, about thirty years old with a trim moustache and a light grey suit, and he looked out of place.

Most of the miracles recounted revolved around relatives who had suddenly and inexplicably recovered from apparently terminal illnesses. One man was so overcome that he couldn't finish his tale, just stood there with the microphone sobbing, while the congregation burst into shouts of 'Hallelujah!'

The preacher took the microphone back to give a sermon. He spoke for a long time about how Jesus the Saviour had come to help those who were lost, a theme which he developed to portray the Manouche as a chosen people. 'Hallelujah!' shouted the crowd as the preacher came to a close.

'Can you feel the Lord?' he demanded. 'Can you feel Him?'

'Yes, yes, I can feel Him!' An old *rom* put his hand up. Several others followed suit while we looked around in consternation.

Chiclo was really trying; his face had an expression of intense concentration.

Tatey nudged him and grinned. 'What am I supposed to feel? I feel the same as when I came in here.'

Chiclo looked up and shrugged. 'Me too, but I wanted to feel something. Maybe next time.'

My lasting impression was that they'd used plastic flowers instead of real ones for the altar.

Mixed-Bloods

The rain came just before the end of September and the nights started closing in. After a dry summer the farmers welcomed the rain, but we didn't. Even if it meant the *vendange* would not be long in coming now, it also meant we were wet all day long. The men especially couldn't stand being confined to the caravans all day, so we moved the fire under a tree and sheltered as best we could, huddling together while Chocote as usual sat on his chair with an umbrella, and the water dripped down our necks and seeped up our trousers and the fire sizzled as it struggled to stay alive.

If it was just for a day it wasn't a problem, but if the rain persisted it wasn't much fun. Without a decent fire the women couldn't cook, so we just ate sandwiches a couple of times a day, and we couldn't dry our clothes. When our jackets got too sodden we'd take them off and hold them over the fire until they steamed, then quickly put them back on; they were still wet, but at least they were warm. Too often we slept in wet clothes as well and children were soon coughing and sneezing, but there was nothing to do except hope for sun the next day, and until that happened we just had to put up with it.

Some days before our harvest was due to begin, Tatey, Django and Passete left, having found work on another chateau nearby, which left just six *rom* in our group apart from myself: Chocote, Beudjeu, Matzo senior, Chiclo, Papi and Claude, a Frenchman married to Dalila's mother Mickey. Claude and Mickey had arrived a few days earlier and pitched a 'bender' tent amongst our caravans, which was a real throw-back because bender tents were what the Gypsies used to live in before even the advent of horse-drawn caravans. Basically a bender tent was a structure of thin bended tree branches, usually hazel for its suppleness, dug into the ground and tied together at the top and then draped with plastic or canvas to keep the rain out.

There was also a French down-and-out called Raymond who Chocote had taken under his wing for some reason. He'd joined us for the last three seasons, a genial man with a gap-toothed grin who needed a large glass of red every morning to steady his hand before he could hold his bowl of coffee.

We went on an outing for a couple of days to pass the time, heading back to the site at Les Billaux to see if there was anyone we knew, but there was just one terribly poor family living in a converted Citroën van which had broken down. We stopped to talk even though we didn't know them, and Chiclo tried to get their van going. While he worked, the family's children, malnourished and with shaved heads, snatched up cigarette butts and then tried to screw off our petrol caps to inhale the fumes. After an hour Chiclo had to admit defeat; the old Citroën's engine didn't even show any sign of turning over. The family was destitute and it was depressing, but there was nothing more we could do and we left.

It was dusk and we made a long diversion on the way back to Fronsac to avoid passing an area notorious for the Mulo. The devil was only supposed to wander during the night, but this place had such a name that we decided to play it safe. Nanoon said he'd seen the Mulo there twice, once in daytime even, and that it had appeared near a small stone bridge where a young boy had been killed years ago.

'It had a long red tongue and bulging eyes and jumped into the road in front of me,' Nanoon had told us. 'I had to swerve. I nearly came off the road.'

When we arrived back at Fronsac we saw three other caravans set well away from our area, and learned that Georges the manager, Monsieur Bigaud, had taken on a group of mixed-blood travellers to fill the gap left by Paquili, Roupenho and Koki. We watched them warily and they watched us back.

'Mixed-bloods can be troublemakers,' Chocote said. 'Not all, but some; they don't have our traditions.' He later shared his misgivings with Georges, who said he'd keep an eye on them, but that we weren't to worry.

'It's not us I'm worried about,' Chocote told him, but Georges said he could hardly tell them to leave now that he'd invited them in.

The *vendange* arrived and it was as always a happy time. We were in the vineyards and cutting and carrying by eight in the morning, and carried on until four or five depending on the light, with an hour off for lunch. We ate well and the wine was free, and we were all soon in good shape, muscles tired at the end of each day. We'd turn in early after some food by the fire, some small talk and guitar-playing and stargazing.

Sundays were a day off, reserved for cleaning up, shaving stubbled checks and trimming bushy moustaches, putting on fresh clothes and visiting friends and relations working on other properties nearby, or receiving visitors ourselves. Either way, the afternoon was a time for partying, and we met all kinds of people: students, holidaymakers, drifters and alternative life seekers, all also working the harvest.

Among the more remarkable were a Dutch couple, he very tall, like many Dutch are, in a big black straw hat that looked like crow's wings, and she big-limbed all over, not as tall as her husband but chunkier, with dark blond hair and red cheeks. He said he'd been in charge of a big textile company in Amsterdam but he'd chucked it in, sold all his belongings and bought a caravan in which he intended to spend the rest of his life. The Manouche were fascinated.

'What about money?' Matzo asked, craning his neck to look up at the Dutchman. 'People keep telling us the *gadjo* live much better than us, more money, nice cars, houses.'

'It's an illusion. What they have are more debts; they are not free. And I don't need more money; I made enough and decided to get out.'

The idea that a rich *gadjo* would turn his back on that world to become a traveller was intriguing in itself to the Manouche, but more mesmerising was the thought of life on the road with unlimited funds.

Then the Dutchman took out a clay pipe which he filled and lit, puffing slowly. 'In my country they are putting all the Gypsies in large camps with fences; different families are forced to live together even if they don't want to. Why, I don't know. It's all about control.'

Chocote was angry; he shook his head in disbelief. 'Everyone else should get together and stamp on Holland, like they did with Germany,' he said.

The Manouche still had bitter memories of the Second World War and what was done to them; it was a topic guaranteed to draw a good audience whenever it was raised.

Oddly, so was the British royal family. I was woken before dawn once because Chocote and Passete were having a furious argument about just how far-reaching the Queen's power was.

'She controls all of England, but only a bit of France,' Chocote said as I poured myself some coffee. 'Isn't that right?'

'Nonsense,' Passete countered, throwing his dregs into the fire. 'She has absolute power over all of England and France, and probably some other places as well.'

'How do you work that out?' Chocote demanded.

'It was her father that freed us from the Germans, wasn't it?'

So we were back to the Germans.

They both turned to me. 'You must know; she's your queen. What do you think?' Chocote said.

'I don't think she has much power anywhere. She's like an institution, a figurehead; she's not the actual government.'

'What do you mean?' Both looked at me in consternation.

'Well, she's the queen of England, Scotland, Wales and Northern Ireland, so four countries, plus she's head of state of lots of others as head of what's called the Commonwealth, but she doesn't really have any actual power.'

Neither Chocote nor Passete could grasp the idea that the Queen had no actual political power.

'So what's the point of her, then?' Chocote asked.

'Like I said, she's kind of an institution. She's head of state but she has no real power.'

'Doesn't make sense,' Passete grunted. 'She's the Queen; she must have power, like our president.'

Trying to explain the idiosyncrasies of the British political system to them was like trying to explain the laws of Pythagoras to a three-year-old, and we soon gave up and poured more coffee and looked forward to the day ahead.

The Vendange

There was always time for relaxation, but we worked hard for Georges; it was the first time he'd taken on Manouche and we wanted to impress him so we would have work the next year. Chocote, Beudjeu and I were the porters, with big buckets strapped to our backs. The cutters emptied their baskets of grapes into our buckets, which we then emptied into a trailer hitched to a tractor. I liked being a porter; it was heavy work but better than bending over the vines all the time, and at the end of each row we could take a rest, smoke a cigarette, pick some figs or apples or drink some water. The children came to the vineyards with us, and the ones who weren't working spent most of their time having grape fights, smearing each other's faces with juice until they were black all over.

Pantoon spent much of his time drooling over a large French Canadian student on a gap year. She wasn't pretty by any stretch of the imagination; her teeth were too big, she looked sort of unbalanced with a big backside combined with small breasts, and her hair was light red and curly. But Pantoon reckoned his chances with her were better than with anyone else, and he used his considerable ingenuity to ensure that he always ended up working next to her.

At the start, Georges sent a few litres of wine to us for lunch every day. It was a nice gesture, but most of us abstained during the working day, so Papi and Raymond cornered the lot. When Raymond fell asleep halfway down a row of grapes, and we didn't discover him snoring gently under the vines until the end of the working day, Chocote told Georges to stop the wine at lunch and send squash instead.

Papi also got himself insensibly drunk one night and wandered over to the caravans of the mixed-blood travellers. It must have been midnight or later, and when Chocote heard about it he immediately sent me and Beudjeu to fetch him back. Papi had gone into the caravan of a woman whose husband was in prison after knifing a *gadjo* at a local dance. He was lucky that she could see he was blind drunk and she didn't call for help or even attack him herself, she just gave him coffee and waited for us to arrive. The next day Chocote sent Papi away to work with Zozo about ten miles from us; he was worried that if the woman's husband came back and heard what had happened he would come looking for Papi.

But Chocote was right that the mixed-bloods could be trouble. A few days later the same woman had a fight in the vineyards. A French girl called her a whore during an argument, which is the worst insult for a Gypsy, and the woman attacked her with her secateurs, stabbing her in the arm and shoulder before she was pulled off and held tight by others from her group. The French girl was screaming – the blood made the wounds look worse than they were – and it wasn't long before she left in an ambulance. Georges was shaken and ordered all of the mixed-bloods off the property.

'You were right; I should have listened to you,' he said to Chocote afterwards. And Papi came back.

*

Nanine gave birth to her seventh child. Matzo had been convinced there could be no birth until well after the *vendange*.

'You're a cannibal,' Chocote said to him when Nanine went into labour and was rushed to hospital in Libourne.

Matzo's rodent features grinned back; he was small and dark and wore a trilby hat. 'It's a full moon, so it'll be a boy.' And it was. Matzo was delighted as he already had four daughters and just two boys, Pantoon and a younger brother, and Nanine was back in the camp cooking for us a day later.

Matzo named Beudjeu as his *kirvo* for the baby, but there was an early scare over the baby's health. It started raining again, so heavily we were soon forced to stop work; the mud clung to our boots and made it impossible for us porters to carry the heavy buckets of grapes up and down the sloping vineyards. It was slippery, dirty and cold, and we were miserable. Baby Beudjeu was kept well wrapped in a cocoon of blankets but caught a chill from the damp air anyway and he felt feverish, hot to the touch.

We took him to a doctor who said he had bronchitis; he looked at him for about one minute and gave Matzo a prescription to reduce the fever and a bill for forty francs. In his hurry, Matzo had left his wallet behind, and the doctor went to take the prescription back. Chiclo, Beudjeu, Claude and I emptied our pockets; we had just forty-two francs between us and we handed over the forty, but we were angry at the doctor in his prim surgery with watercolours on the walls and magazines to leaf through. By threatening to take back the prescription despite our need he'd tried to humiliate us, and we hated him for that.

'Fuck him,' Chiclo spat when we were outside. 'We might be poor but we've got our pride too, and we'll always survive and stay free because we rely on no one, just ourselves.'

Most importantly, young Beudjeu made a quick recovery.

*

It rained heavily for two days and we were sodden again. Chocote was downcast and ready to leave but didn't because he'd given his word that we'd work until the end of the *vendange*.

'He's a good *gadjo*,' he said from under his umbrella while the rest of us shivered. 'And I don't want to break my word, not if we want to come back next year.'

And everyone else stayed because Chocote stayed.

While we waited for the rain to stop we went to see Passete, although Chiclo didn't come. Passete had a good place, just three caravans inside the courtyard of a chateau with a covered area which had long wooden tables and benches, where we were able to eat together out of the rain. Chocote helped himself to a few plants from the garden to take back to Oumlo, but on the return to Fronsac we had an unpleasant shock.

Just after we crossed the river coming out of Libourne we saw the blue lights of police cars turning ahead, and as we drew closer we could see there'd been an accident, then that one of the cars was Chiclo's brown and white Simca, badly dented and half on the verge. It was still drizzling, making it foul driving weather, and we feared the worst, but as Beudjeu pulled over we couldn't see any injured and there was no sign of an ambulance. We spotted Chiclo; he was shouting at a thin middle-aged *gadjo* who had a sour expression, and Pantoon and Niglo were nearby, standing with clenched fists. Then we saw Dalila and Nanine with baby Beudjeu, and Chiclo's children, Bimbo and Choca, and Mooka too; the Simca must have been packed and it was a miracle nobody had been hurt.

The two cars were on opposite sides of the road and Chiclo's had come off worse; the engine seemed to have been damaged. Steam rose from under the raised bonnet. The *gadjo* stank of wine.

'He was on the wrong side of the road; if I hadn't swerved we'd have hit head on!' Chiclo waved his arm angrily at the man and spat. 'And he's been drinking.'

The police weren't really interested; no one had been hurt and we were Manouche, so why bother? Chiclo took the *gadjo's* address and they filled in their insurance forms, not that it did any good. Without witnesses and a breath test it was one man's word against another, and Chiclo never got anything back. Somehow, though, the Simca was coaxed back into life and limped back to our site, so at least Chiclo wasn't homeless.

*

One more baby was born before the end of the *vendange*, a girl this time for Tatey's wife Marguerite, who was Volka's elder sister. Again I was asked to be *kirvo*, and again I accepted. They named her Vita, like Passete's wife.

They were working nearby but weren't happy. 'We're not allowed a break even for a cigarette, and there's no wine,' Tatey grumbled. 'The patron is just mean. I don't want to work for him any more.'

So they left before the harvest was finished and returned to Le Dorat in the Limoges, which meant I had three baptisms outstanding. Tatey was a very superstitious man, though, and he didn't like the idea of a delay to his new daughter's baptism.

'Beng and other evil spirits can enter an unbaptised child,' he said, pulling on his drooping moustache. 'If that happens she will become one of them, an evil spirit wandering the earth.'

Marguerite sat up all night to ward off the evil spirits and if baby Vita cried a lot, her mother said that was because evil spirits were trying to enter. 'She needs to be baptised before she can sleep properly,' she said.

'Until a baby is baptised it isn't properly alive,' Tatey added, and we agreed that one of his brothers should take my place at the ceremony and we'd have a celebration feast some other day.

*

The rain eased and we finished the *vendange* in double-quick time. Everybody was in holiday mood, and Georges invited us all to eat together for an end-of-harvest feast. This hadn't happened in years, certainly not in my time, although Chocote said he'd once worked for a very kind man in Saint-Émilion who had always put on a party. Even so, he was uneasy this time.

'French meals go on too long, and we have to use knives and forks and different plates for different food,' he said. He was worried that he'd be embarrassed.

Chocote asked Georges if we could just have the food sent over to our camp so we could eat in private and then join everyone afterwards, but Georges wouldn't hear of it. 'You are my guests, of course we'll eat together,' he said, and Chocote had no option but to accept with good grace.

The dinner was held in an outhouse next to the wine cellars. A long wooden table with benches had been set for about fifty people, plates, knives, forks and spoons and even napkins. It looked like our worst fears were about to be realised and we were to be subjected to one of those French food marathons, when everyone has to sit for hours with long waits between courses. We were more used to putting all the food out at once and grabbing what we wanted without waiting around; even a big meal was usually over within fifteen or twenty minutes.

That meant most of us overdid the first couple of courses and were soon full and anxious to leave the table, but the wine was good. In time we relaxed and stood from the hard benches, wandering around and snacking as the meat was brought in, and then a whole suckling pig that had been spit-roasted arrived; even those who were full soon found more room for that.

Georges also stood and came to talk to us, and his wife joined us too. They asked a lot of questions about the Manouche and seemed genuinely interested.

'A pity there aren't more like him,' Chocote said.

Some had trouble with the knives and forks, but Pantoon just took his meat in his hand and ate as he was used to. Georges' eyebrows went up a bit, but he was too polite to say anything and turned back to resume his conversation with Claude. He was intrigued that a Frenchman had decided to marry into the Manouche.

'How did they accept you?' Georges asked.

'Like one of their own.' Claude pushed back his mane of light brown hair. 'I met my wife Mickey during a *vendange*. We don't have much, but we are happy.'

'What about you?' Georges turned to me.

'I also feel I belong; I've got three godchildren already! It's a very close community, and they are very protective of each other.'

'You'll come back next year?'

'We'll come back for sure. Chocote can tell you where to contact us.'

Pantoon, meanwhile, having finished his pork and cleaned his hands, had managed to manoeuvre himself alongside the French Canadian girl. The more he drank, the bolder his advances became, until he was openly cuddling her and squeezing her thighs under the table, but she didn't seem to mind. She'd probably never had such an ardent admirer before.

Django and a cousin of Tatey showed up halfway through the evening, and Georges had extra places set for them. The wine was replaced with sweet yellow Muscat, and a huge chocolate cake covered in hot sauce was brought in. The Manouche didn't really go in for cake making and we all wanted to make pigs of ourselves, except we'd overeaten and could barely take another mouthful; all except for Claude, who'd been keeping himself for the dessert and calmly ate his way through five helpings while we looked on ruefully.

With the meal over, it was time to party. Pantoon accompanied Chocote on guitar, and Tatey's cousin had the most amazing voice; he sang from the depths of his soul and everyone, Gypsy and French alike, was entranced.

In the middle of all this, Claude put on a show of fire breathing, spitting out long jets of pure alcohol spirit and igniting them with a burning torch, lighting up the hall in a lurid glare.

Chocote turned to Georges with a grin. 'You see? We are artists!'

And while Claude breathed fire and Pantoon kept playing, the party continued until well after midnight, before we wandered back to our camp and the fire. Some began to drift off to bed until there were just three or four of us left, and the last thing I remember is Matzo singing a sad song as Pantoon accompanied him. It was a beautiful picture, the father down on one knee, hand on chest, his head tilted back as his son stood above him with his guitar in the night, just the smallest glow still coming from the fire.

Paquili in the rain, *vendange* 1979.

Departures

The day after the end-of-*vendange* party, we were hungover and subdued. Georges paid us our money at around midday and gave us a couple of crates of good wine, and repeated his invitation for us to return the next year. We made a trip into Libourne to buy presents and food, drink some cold beers and generally enjoy the sensation of having a pocketful of banknotes. Then we visited friends and relatives in the area to make our farewells before returning to Fronsac to pack, ready for an early departure the next morning, and spent a quiet evening reminiscing over the year's events.

We rose at dawn and were soon ready to leave. Papi was going with Zozo and Lachi back to Le Dorat in the horse-drawn caravan; they would stay in the region for winter, eking out an existence, while the rest of us were headed back to Marseille. The Manouche didn't make a great fuss of farewells in general, but it was different when it was to be for the whole winter; there was always the thought that we might not meet again. We embraced and kissed cheeks, and some had tears in their eyes.

'We'll be together again in the spring!' Chiclo called out, climbing into his battered Simca with Dalila and revving the engine. '*Ya la*, let's go!'

I went with Beudjeu, Blon and Pesi in their Renault, and Chocote was already in his Saviem with Oumlo, Niglo and Pepite. It felt sad and desolate, the travelling season was over for another year, but it had been a good summer and there would be others.

We threaded our way back across France, southwest to southeast, past Toulouse, the Pyrenees to our right this time, and around Mont-pellier. Nobody spoke much, everyone was lost in their own thoughts, and we pulled up in front of Chocote's small house late at night. Next door the lights were on and Paquili came out to greet us, then Roupenho and Koki, young Matzo and Volka, and all the other women, and soon we were drinking coffee, swapping tales and catching up on everyone's news.

'You should have seen the feast the patron put on for us,' Pantoon said, strumming his guitar with Roupenho accompanying. He described the chocolate cake and hot sauce. 'The best I've ever had; you should have been there!'

'Next year,' Koki said, darting a glance at Tac-Tac, who apparently still hadn't forgiven him.

'Well, they said we could go back next year, and we missed your guitar. But let me tell you about this *gadje*, big girl, lots to hold on to.' Pantoon grinned cheekily, flicking his long hair back from his face.

And so it went on until we finally drifted off to bed.

The next day was like the first day back after a holiday. We shopped, the women cleaned, and Chocote gave his picket fence another coat of green paint while Paquili's old father looked on and wondered if he should do the same. We also arranged the baptism of Volka's baby Nadjo in a nearby church where the priest was familiar with the Manouche.

It was a simple affair, no prayers or hymns, just a blessing and the sprinkling of holy water and a short sermon from the priest, a small beady-eyed man, forty or fifty years old with greying hair and wire-rimmed spectacles. Then he shook all our hands, and as *kirvo* I went to buy food and wine and beer for a small celebration back at the houses.

I stayed for another week or so, then it was time to take the train back to London to find some work for winter, and again the farewells were emotional. We promised to see each other in the spring, but the whole way back I felt confused; it was a huge wrench and I was about to become a *gadjo* again.

*

London was hard. Again I worked night shifts, as many as I could, and again rarely saw people, sleeping by day, then waking and making my way to Broadcasting House to filter the news until the next morning. After a breakfast of hot milk with a splash of whisky and a raw egg whipped in, it was back to bed again.

I was staying again in Eddy's house in south London, which had been christened *the Night Control Centre* with a sign we found in a disused council building. Apart from Eddy and Theresa, his Sardinian wife, there was also a Portuguese photographer, Paulo, and his Turkish girl-friend staying, along with a regular stream of visitors from all over the world. Word seemed to have got around and there were visitors from Australia, South America and the United States, some of whom stopped for a few days, others who hung around for a couple of weeks or more. Drunks and drug users also knocked on the door to see if the house was some sort of shelter, but probably the strangest guest was a fringe member of the Red Army Faction from Munich who brought his eleven-year-old daughter along and said the German police were looking for him. He tried to get us to join him in passionate political debates and he couldn't understand our lack of interest.

'But we must fight capitalism, we need a revolution, it's the only way!' He slapped his hand on the kitchen table, looking around and challenging anyone to take him up. His name was Klaus and he was a thin man with lank fair hair over a balding patch, full of nervous energy.

'I'm going to roll a joint.' Alan, another Londoner and a recent addition to the household, rose from the table and sauntered off.

'And I'm going out to take some photographs,' said Portuguese Paulo, who was working on a project to photograph all the remaining public toilets in London before they were decommissioned.

Klaus was bemused; we were more interested in sport or photography or music or almost anything rather than politics. Back in Munich, he said, they would start every day with a fierce political debate, but after a week he seemed to relax.

'It's very good here,' he said one day when we were in the garden, which was thick with the scent of honeysuckle. 'Really, I like it. My daughter too is happier. Maybe it's better this way.'

Christmas and New Year came and went. I visited my father in Reading briefly; it had been more than three years since my mother had passed away already, and my sister came over from the United States, and we ate and drank too much, like most people, and imagined we were enjoying ourselves.

My father, a retired army officer, was still mystified by my intent to go back to the Gypsies. 'Why can't you get a proper job like other people?'

'I've had proper jobs. I want to try different things while I still can, while I'm not tied down.'

'Never could tell you anything,' he grunted, taking another sip of his gin and It, a mixture of one part gin and two parts sweet martini, with one of those cocktail cherries in it.

By March I was thin and pale, picking up the sobriquet *sick dog* from others in the house, but I had saved enough money to begin planning my return to Marseille, and bought a slightly battered Simca estate from a car auction by Wandsworth Bridge. The passenger door had been badly dented, but it had a low mileage and the engine seemed good, and it was just big enough to sleep in. A month later I was ready, and again bade everyone farewell and retraced my journey to the south of France.

On the ferry from Dover to Calais I again spent the entire time on deck, sucking in the sea air and sloughing off those months of night shifts. Why would I want to do that full-time? I was tense with excitement and anticipation and realised again how much I had missed the Manouche.

The Last Harvest

I arrived back to a raucous welcome and the customary big party and immediately felt at home in a way I hadn't in London. Little had changed, although Paquili's father had died and Paquili and Nina had moved into the house next to Chocote, while Ghuno stayed in her caravan parked alongside. Everyone else was still there, and Chiclo laughed when he saw my Simca.

'Now you are really Manouche,' he said, popping the bonnet and examining the engine. 'It looks okay, but if it breaks down I can always use the parts.'

Beudjeu and Pesi had a daughter and took me as *kirvo*.

I had no idea where this was going and flirted briefly with the thought of staying full-time, buying a caravan and taking a Manouche wife, but deep inside I knew that was unlikely. Apart from anything else the French authorities would soon be on my back, I wouldn't qualify for a house, and I wouldn't get the treasured social security payments. The prospect of spending the rest of my life living off scraps from the dumps was not especially alluring.

As it was, I spent four *vendanges* and three years with the Manouche, following the same cycle, wintering in London, and living with Chocote and his company from spring until the harvest. The routine rarely altered, but even so, little by little, things were changing. The last year we didn't even go to Les Saintes; everyone agreed it had been taken over by the tourists.

'It's wrong. We're like animals in a zoo,' Paquili stormed, echoing Beja's complaints from a couple of years before.

Chiclo snorted. 'I wouldn't pay to see you.'

Georges welcomed us back in Lugon, but it was to be our last *vendange* there as well.

'I'm sorry,' he said, and he looked it, 'but we will also go over to machines next year. Everyone is doing it except the very special vine-yards which will still be picked by hand, and they are few.'

'I suppose it's the way of the world,' I said, 'but it's sad too.'

'It is. They call it progress, but I sometimes wonder if it is.'

Again he put on a huge spread for us at the end and again we ate and sang and danced by the fireside, but already there was a different mood. Other groups of Manouche in the area had been given the same news; they wouldn't be needed the next year either. The days of the hand-picked *vendange* were drawing to a close.

I drove back to London straight from Bordeaux, taking the overnight ferry from Saint-Malo to Portsmouth this time and booking a single cabin, but instead of sleeping spent most of the time playing blackjack, winning hugely for a couple of hours, then losing the lot again. The Simca had held up surprisingly well and soon I was back at the Night Control Centre, still smelling of woodsmoke and tobacco.

Eddy and Theresa were expecting their first baby and people were moving out of their rented rooms in the Night Control Centre to give them some space. I stayed until their son Simon was born, then rented a basement flat in Chelsea. It was more than I could afford, so I had to go back to work, this time freelancing at Bush House, at that time a Tower of Babel of radio broadcasting, transmitting to the world in dozens of languages and employing people of every colour and reli-gion; even the canteen offered food from all around the world. It was more interesting than Broadcasting House and attracted a different breed of journalist. Maybe it was just gentler.

Either way, *life* took over and it would be some years before I saw the Manouche again. That winter I met my first wife, Monica, a Colom-bian studying music in Cambridge. In what seemed like the blink of an eye we were married and had our first son, Daniel, and I had accepted a full-time position at Bush House and taken out a mortgage on a flat overlooking Clapham Common.

Beudjeu and I were writing to each other every two or three months, simple letters to say 'we are well' and 'how is everyone?' or 'the weather here is such and such', but I couldn't hope to convey what was happening to me, and then we moved to Colombia.

I'd stumbled across a small television news agency called UPITN, and they taught me how to use a 16mm camera and how to change the film by touch in a portable black bag. Above all they agreed a small monthly guarantee, enough to cover our rent, and more generous payments per story used on top. I also picked up agreements for on-use payments from BBC radio, the *Daily Telegraph*, ABC Australia and CBC in Canada. It seemed more attractive than the daily drudgery of commuting, so we packed, rented out the flat in Clapham and left.

And it was mostly good. With two or more syndicated stories a week we could afford a large apartment with a maid just on the affluent north side of Bogotá – the city was divided between the rich in the north and the poor in the south – and a beaten-up Renault 4, which we used to explore the surrounding country. It wasn't long before our second son, another Simon, was born.

It was a good time for news there, but not safe. The El Salvador peace talks were being conducted in Bogotá, guerrillas from groups like the FARC, M-19 and ELN were very active, and on top of that it was the heyday of the narco kings. Cocaine production was going through the roof and people like Pablo Escobar and Carlos Lehder held sway.

It was a small world; I interviewed President Betancur, dined with the Justice Minister, Lara Bonilla, on the night of his assassination, and went to Lehder's house for a drug-fuelled celebration after he formed a political party. He's probably still doing time in a US prison after eventually getting extradited.

I also had contacts within M-19 and the drugs business, and both tripped me up, the first when M-19 tried to storm the 7th Brigade's headquarters in the jungle town of Caquetá, deep in the southeast. I flew down and was in time to film a row of maybe thirty bodies laid out in the town square which the army said were guerrillas, even though some locals said they were just other locals caught in the crossfire. They also said a helicopter had been brought down, which the army denied.

Either way the 7th Brigade weren't happy to see my camera and frogmarched me to their barracks, checking my shoulders for strap bruises which might come from carrying a backpack, one way they decided who was a guerrilla and who was not, and they destroyed my film. They also held me in a cell for two days of questioning, before putting me on an aeroplane back to Bogotá after the union of international journalists intervened.

Much more serious was when I was commissioned to cover a story which would show that the government's much-vaunted use of pesticides on marijuana plantations was a failure. The pesticides killed everything, including crops of potatoes, maize and coffee; the peasant farmers hated them, but most of the marijuana plantations were well hidden in the jungle and supply was barely affected. With the *Time* magazine correspondent Tom Quinn, I went to film a house in the lawless southern slums of Bogotá which was packed to the gunnels with bales of marijuana. My car was covered in press stickers and I had even taken Daniel along with me, strapped into his baby seat; it was supposed to be a safe prearranged shoot. We had barely started filming when car horns started bleating outside and half a dozen officers from F-2, Colombia's specialist anti-drug unit, burst in. Everyone was arrested.

'What do we do with the gringos?' asked a junior officer.

'I hate fucking gringos; let's do them,' the captain, a thin-lipped man holding a pistol, snapped viciously.

'What about the kid?'

'We have institutions for kids like that.'

Fortunately a sympathetic officer took down the number of my brother-in-law Gato and went to call him, and he was soon at the station to collect Daniel.

First we endured two days and a night at F-2's headquarters, separated and sitting in straight-backed chairs and repeatedly being told to sign our 'confessions', except there was nothing to confess. Fortunately I'd kept the telex assigning me to the story. We weren't allowed to sleep, no food was provided, and further down the corridor we could hear the shouts and screams of other prisoners being physically abused. Again the journalists' union came to the rescue and I had a visit from the British consul. He was friendly and sympathetic, but not a lot of use beyond guaranteeing I would be properly looked after and treated fairly. Tom had less success with the American embassy; they didn't send someone until much later.

We were transferred to the notorious *La Modelo* prison, better known as *La Universidad Blanco*, the 'White University', a sprawling white-walled high-security complex to the south of the city, where we were welcomed by the director, a genial grey-haired man in a cardigan with a large marijuana plant in a pot behind his desk.

We were put into a special wing for a small number of *celebrity* prisoners. We each had our own cell and could order a bed to be made and buy blankets, and we could eat at the various food concessions which operated inside the prison. It really was like a microcosm of the outside world. There were the food stalls, a laundry, a pool table, hairdressers; pretty much everything was available if you could afford it. The poorer prisoners slept in a heap to keep warm in cells holding thirty or forty people together and scooped their food with their hands from the prison cauldrons which passed through twice a day. I'm not sure either Tom or I would have survived that for very long.

We were sharing our wing with a gang accused of stealing £13 million from the Colombian Defence Ministry's bank account in London, so, despite being roused for a cold shower at six every morning, we were relatively comfortable. We had a television with VHS player and an exercise bicycle, and could go out into the main courtyard whenever we wanted. But losing one's freedom is a harsh experience, and seeing Monica and Daniel and Simon through mesh wire was deeply unsettling. I would spend hours sleeping, shutting out the nightmare.

It was a big story in the local media, crews and reporters regularly came in to interview us, and we were dubbed the *narco periodistas*, the narco journalists. True to form, the BBC frantically backed away from me, but UPITN dispatched their New York bureau chief, a fearsome Frenchwoman called Colette Dumez, to Bogotá. She remains one of my dearest friends.

There was no evidence against either of us except our presence in the house of grass, and I could prove I'd been assigned to the story. Ten days of Colette bending his ear was enough to persuade the colonel in charge of my case to finally see sense and sign my release papers.

In all I'd spent six weeks in *La Modelo*, but Tom was not so lucky. Like the BBC, *Time* magazine adopted a hands-off approach and he ended up serving three months before being freed. There was no *habeas corpus* in Colombia at the time; the country was under emergency rule and any suspect could be held for six months without charge.

The experience had shaken me, and then I started getting phone calls with death threats and decided that after three years the Colombian adventure was over. It's a stunningly beautiful country, but it was going through a bad time.

When Tom did eventually get out, he and his wife Zuma were killed in a road accident within weeks. I'd already left the country, but former colleagues in Bogotá claimed the accident was suspicious. They left behind three young daughters.

A Holiday

Back in London again, UPITN, soon to become WTN (Worldwide Television News) when we lost the ITN stake, gave me a desk job. I felt trapped even though it was an amazing little company to work for. We were the cowboys of the broadcast news industry; all the mainstream media looked down on us, but at the same time were totally reliant on us. If there was an earthquake in Japan or a train wreck in India, it was the agencies that supplied the pictures, and at that time there was only two of us, WTN and Reuters.

Everyone was very friendly; John McCarthy was one of the first to come and shake my hand and welcome me to the team. It was a tight-knit group with none of the ego problems that you get in the broadcasters, and we specialised in very long lunches at the local Turkish restaurant Efes, or the Crown and Sceptre pub across the road.

But the easygoing atmosphere was shattered the day John McCarthy was kidnapped in Beirut. It was his first foreign assignment and he'd broken all the ground rules. It had been drummed into him that if things turned sour he should attach himself to a seasoned international hack and cross the road when they did, and on no account should he get too close to the locals. John had apparently taken a Palestinian girlfriend, and when serious fighting broke out and all the international journalists went to the Commodore hotel in East Beirut, where they were protected by Druze militiamen, John took a backroad for the airport, where he was picked up by Shia fighters. He spent five years in captivity.

Before he was released, we'd moved to Switzerland and were back in touch with the Manouche. A charming but slightly eccentric Swiss entrepreneur called John Winistoerfer, who had married into one of Zurich's wealthiest families, had decided that what the country needed was an international television business channel, broadcast in English and German: EBC, the European Business Channel. It was never going to work, and it didn't, but it was fun while it lasted.

Winistoerfer, or Wini as he became known, was a slim and cheerful man, always dapper and with too much optimism for his own good, along with a taste for fine dining and wines, and he made the big mistake of hiring in expensive known broadcasters from television stations long before we were ready to go on air. The editor was the left-wing commentator Will Hutton, and he brought in people such as Ed Mitchell, ITN's business correspondent, and James Long, Ed's counterpart from the BBC, and half a dozen others, all on big salaries. He paid little or no attention to the German side, assuming that as we were in German-speaking Zurich we could find all the talent we needed locally. I was the lowest paid of the British contingent and had been brought in as operations director because, as an agency person, I was the only one who actually understood how to move pictures around the world.

'So how did you do it at the BBC?' I asked Will.

'We called the BBC SPUR and they did it for us,' he said. The SPUR was their satellite bookings office.

'We haven't got a SPUR; we have to do it ourselves.'

Then our distribution satellite was lost when the Ariane rocket carrying it blew up. So we had a staff of more than one hundred, many of them on six-figure salaries, and nowhere to broadcast.

We managed to get a breakfast slot on German broadcaster RTL, but it wasn't sustainable, and the situation was made worse because by all accounts the Germans were falling around laughing at the peculiar Swiss German accent of our 'German' presenters. We had to go back to the market and spend heavily to bring in 'real' German speakers.

At the first chance, Monica and I drove the relatively short distance down to Marseille with the boys. It was Monica's first visit to the Manouche and I hadn't seen them for years, but little had changed. Chocote's was still the best-kept house. Beudjeu was still at Mirabeau, and his daughter, now named Monique, had grown into a beautiful young girl with thick wavy hair which fell past her shoulders; she had inherited Pesi's chocolate-coloured eyes. But there were no more harvests and the company was pretty much stuck in Marseille all year round. Chocote's predictions were coming true.

Despite this, it was a happy reunion. Monica and the boys were enthralled, and we stayed several days before returning to Zurich, taking back memories of the braziers and duelling guitars at night. I swore to myself that we wouldn't lose contact again, but eventually we did, and finding them again wasn't to prove easy.

Within two years EBC had gone bankrupt. It hadn't occurred to me that companies *did* go bankrupt in Switzerland. Will Hutton didn't even stay that long; after persuading so many people to join him in Switzerland, within a year he had quickly scuttled off back to London when he was offered a job on the *Guardian* newspaper. Some of us felt that as 'captain' he should have stayed on the bridge instead of being first off the sinking ship. But then the offer of a place on a lifeboat must have been tempting.

The sharks started circling as CNN, Reuters, Time Warner and others mulled over buying the operation. I had become close to Winistoerfer and he put me on his due diligence team, and in the following weeks, as we picked over the entrails of EBC, I learned how businesses actually worked. It's true that you can learn more from failure than success, and I decided to make a career change. I wanted to be a start-up specialist.

No one bought the company, mostly due to the Swiss government refusing to allow a foreign company to buy more than forty-nine percent, a real case of cutting off your nose to spite your face. They later realised that and they changed the ownership laws, but too late for us.

Many of the staff moved to EBN, European Business News, a new start-up funded by American entrepreneurs in London, and it eventually morphed into CNBC when America's NBC took it over. So maybe Wini's original concept wasn't so bad after all; he'd just got the business plan or timing wrong. And at least the Swiss were honourable about the redundancy payments, even if after just two years they weren't huge.

We went back to Marseille for one last time before returning to London, but it wasn't a happy visit. Chocote had banished Beudjeu for six months to a field some ten miles out of the city after he had confessed to having an affair. Beudjeu didn't argue about his punishment; he'd brought shame on his father and family. We went to visit him and Pesi and young Monique and stayed a couple of nights in their field, sleeping crammed into the back of our Renault Espace. Beudjeu was downcast.

'I was stupid,' he said, shaking his head and scuffing at the ground. 'Who will look up to me now?'

'Time heals everything,' I told him. 'And I have an idea: let us take Monique on a small holiday so you can spend time with Pesi on your own.'

'A holiday?' he said, looking at me questioningly. The Manouche weren't really familiar with the idea of holidays.

"Yes, we'll go to the Camargue and rent a boat for a week. I don't have any work, there's no rush for us. And we'll look after her. It'll be an experience.'

Monique was beside herself with excitement, and the next day Pesi dressed her in her best clothes, a blue denim smock with red pullover, and packed a small bag, and we set off. We spent the following week drifting lazily across the waters of the Camargue, and stopped for two nights in the lovely town of Arles where we wandered the streets, young Monique agog, staring in the shop windows. Twice we ate in a restaurant, steaks for the children, *moules frites* for me and Monica.

On other evenings we just pulled in and moored by the canal banks and cooked ourselves a simple meal. It was beautiful countryside, a wetland paradise full of pink flamingos and wild white horses, and Daniel and Simon accepted Monique easily in the way that children do. On a boat everyone has to pull their weight; maybe that's what makes it so relaxing, the constant activity as we passed through locks juxtaposed with the complete peace of the surroundings.

'We ate in a restaurant!' Monique announced breathlessly when we returned to the field outside Marseille a week later.

'You did?'

'Yes, there was a tablecloth and real napkins and we used knives and forks.'

'And what did you eat there?' Beudjeu asked, laughing, but Pesi looked a bit doubtful. The Manouche never ate in restaurants.

'Steak frites, of course, and then ice cream, two helpings; it was delicious!'

While we'd been away, Beudjeu had been to see Chocote and begged him to let them return to Mirabeau, and his father had finally relented, saying he could come back at the end of the month, just a week away.

'You'll behave yourself this time?' I asked.

'Of course; he won't give me another chance if I mess up again. He's a softie at heart, but he can be tough when he needs to be.'

Being the son of the head of the company meant that Beudjeu was under especial scrutiny.

We stayed another night with them in the field. It felt very alone under the stars, a small fire burning the only light visible, and I could see that Pesi still hadn't quite forgiven Beudjeu.

The following morning we rose early and, after coffee and more tearful farewells, headed north, back towards England again.

A Gadjo Again

I drifted again and was soon back in Switzerland, this time in Lugano in the Italian-speaking south of the country, where I was tasked with relaunching a general entertainment channel, Telecampione, and turning it into a business news channel. I was quickly learning that there were a limited number of start-up specialists in the world of broadcasting.

The station took its name from its location, a small Italian enclave near Lugano called Campione, which allowed us to broadcast into the Milan and Venice areas of Italy without a Swiss licence. Our signal didn't reach further. It also allowed me to pay regular visits to the Manouche; a long weekend was enough to make the return journey. Although the welcomes were as warm as ever, there was a deep sadness about the little rows of houses by then. Chocote and Oumlo were growing old, and Paquili and the others weren't happy with the enforced sedentary life.

'We're just second-class citizens.' Beudjeu shrugged his shoulders. 'We're still Manouche, but we don't really travel any more; there's nowhere to go and no work except the dumps.'

I also felt more of an outsider; I was clean-shaven and wore clean clothes and had a nice car, and I felt they could sense that I was no longer really a traveller and had embraced the *gadjo* way of life.

On the plus side, the two young Nadjos and young Monique were growing fast and were healthy and full of life. I was still their *kirvo*, and always bought plenty of food and wine for the company when I went down. Koki and Pantoon still brought out their guitars, and as always we sat out long into the night listening to music, reminiscing about the old days.

Back in Lugano, we bought the EBC archive and did our best on a minimal budget, but it was soon clear that business television didn't attract big audiences, as least not in Italy, and the owner, Dr Giovanni Casella, a jolly and rotund man who loved his food, soon reverted to light entertainment game shows and scantily dressed hostesses. The audiences went up again, but once more after less than two years I was out of a job.

Surprisingly WTN took me back and made me their vice president for Europe, tasked with capturing the new markets offered by the collapse of the former Soviet Union. I criss-crossed Eastern Europe, Russia, the Baltic states, Kazakhstan, Tajikistan, Uzbekistan, all the way to Vladivostok in Siberia, and corner the market we did, or at least eighty percent of it; Reuters were very slow off the mark. But I ignored my own advice to Beudjeu to behave himself in his marriage, for it was during this time that in Moscow I met and fell in love with a beautiful green-eyed Tartar, Zoulfia, who was to become my second wife after Monica and I were divorced. I don't care what anyone says; I don't think there is such a thing as a happy divorce, even if many years later we managed to become friends again.

Zoulfia and I soon had a daughter, Nikita. We lived in a small flat in south London while I commuted by motorbike to WTN's new offices, an old gin warehouse in Camden on the other side of the river, at least when I was not sitting on a decrepit Tupolev or Yak-40 and staying in run-down hotels in frozen countries across the old USSR.

Then the Associated Press of America bought WTN and it became APTN, and all of WTN's senior management were let go, all except for me. They wanted the revenue I represented, so I had a stay of execution. Instead they put me in charge of subscription revenue across the world, apart from the USA. So the travels continued, now also to Japan, China, Australia, New Zealand, South America and the Middle East. APTN's revenues doubled and the money was good, but I wasn't happy with the culture of the company any more. It wasn't fun in the way it had been, and I became a thorn in the side of the Americans now running the show.

I remember one management meeting with visiting dignitaries from

AP's New York headquarters, when one of the Americans ripped into the latest Palestinian suicide bombing in Israel.

'I don't agree with terrorism,' I said, stupidly thinking this was a rational discussion. 'But I can understand why despair and hopelessness might drive someone to do that. I mean, even if you have a university degree, if there's no hope, what do you do?'

The Americans railed at me, calling me a terrorist sympathiser and a lot more besides. I was dumbfounded, but the writing was on the wall, and it wasn't long before our managing director, Ian Ritchie, called me into his office. Ritchie was a clever and charming but also ambitious Yorkshireman with his sights set on high society, who somehow went on to become head of the All England tennis club, then of the English Rugby Football Union and then of the English rugby premiership.

'We have to let you go. You'll get a month's salary. Don't think you can claim more; you're not in a union, you know,' Ritchie told me, jigging his legs up and down nervously, which he did all the time.

'Read my contract and I'll see you tomorrow.' I stood and left his office.

'You know he comes from the wrong side of the rail tracks in Bradford,' another employee from Yorkshire observed.

'It never occurred to me that there was a *right* side of the tracks in a place like Bradford,' I replied.

My contract stipulated a minimum of six months' pay, and to be fair Ritchie quickly and sheepishly acknowledged his mistake and even went so far as to throw a lavish party complete with a live band to bid me farewell.

I wasn't bothered by this development; we'd had enough of life in our cramped flat and were planning to move to the south of Spain, where we were building a kind of concrete igloo with swimming pool. To the front of our plot we could see the Mediterranean and behind the snowy peaks of the Sierra Nevada; it seemed an idyllic place, although in the end it turned out that our Belgian estate agent and builder was crooked. He built the house, but he didn't actually own the land, so we lost everything we'd invested. The house is still standing there on its hillside like some kind of twenty-first-century folly, over-grown and uninhabitable. But, just as it seemed we were staring into an abyss, Lady Fortune came to our rescue once more.

Unbeknownst to anyone, for the previous couple of months I had been talking to a sheikh from Qatar about their long-promised launch of an English version of Al Jazeera, the Arabic channel which had been sending shockwaves across the Middle East with its fearless reporting on the Palestinian intifada and the second Iraq war. I'd been introduced to them by Riz Khan, then a presenter with CNN, who had extensive contacts in the Gulf. Their reporting so enraged the Americans that President George W Bush had even threatened to bomb their Doha headquarters, and their correspondent in Baghdad was killed in what looked like a targeted attack by USAF jets on their offices there. The Americans denied it was deliberate, but Al Jazeera had given them the coordinates of the office just to avoid such an attack.

I was sent on a final tour of the Far East to introduce my successor at APTN, a British Sri Lankan with the improbable name of Daisy, to my contacts at the various broadcasters. The last stop was Seoul, and it was there that I received a phone call telling me to go to the Qatar Airways office, where a ticket was waiting to take me to Doha. I told Daisy that I was distressed by leaving APTN, and that instead of returning straight to London I wanted to visit Zoulfia in Moscow, where she was in turn visiting her mother with Nikita.

Daisy duly left, and as soon as she was out of the way I went down-town to collect my new ticket. Not only was it there, but it was first class. I'd never flown first class in my life before!

I took a taxi to Seoul airport in the early hours of the morning. Bizarrely the driver was a huge Bob Marley fan, and we drove through the silent city listening to 'Buffalo Soldier' and 'Exodus' and 'Three Little Birds' at full volume while my mind whirled with the possibilities.

The heat in Doha hit me like a brick wall as soon as the aircraft doors opened. I'd been to nearby Dubai before, but in winter, and this was already late spring. A chauffeur-driven BMW collected me from the aeroplane steps, and after being fast-tracked through immigration I was driven to the Ritz-Carlton hotel and was told I would receive a call later. In my room, I drew the heavy curtains, ramped up the air conditioning, and fell deeply asleep.

It was only a few hours later that the telephone clattered into life, but it felt like I'd been asleep all day and most of the night. I was told to be ready within the hour. I drew back the curtains and blinding sunlight flooded in; it was still the afternoon of the same day. Within the hour I'd showered, breakfasted from room service and dressed in the only lightweight suit I had, and I went to wait under the enormous chandelier which dominated the cavernous lobby.

It wasn't long before I was approached by a man who introduced himself as Mahmoud Bouneb, the head of Al Jazeera's children's channel. He was a close confident of Sheikh Hamad bin Thamer Al Thani, chairman of the Al Jazeera board and a member of the Al Thani dynasty which ruled the tiny but fabulously wealthy country.

Mahmoud was a Tunisian, a big man with a thin moustache and dressed in slacks, linen jacket and open-necked shirt, and as we drove in his Land Cruiser to Al Jazeera's compound he chatted about life in Qatar.

'It's hot, it's dusty and there's not a lot to do sometimes, but it's a good life for an expat: no tax, good schools, and it's easy to make friends.' His English was fluent, barely accented.

'Sounds good to me.'

'When you get to see the sheikh, don't talk too much, listen, and he'll want to know you can make this channel work for $100 million dollars a year, no more. Better if it's just under.'

'I can do that.' I was later to learn that the Qataris didn't really focus on the odd million dollars here and there; what really caught their attention were the pennies.

We met in Sheikh Hamad's office; he was a small, almost timid man with a narrow, pinched face, crooked teeth, and immaculate white robes. His command of English was poor, and Mahmoud translated as he asked the questions I'd been primed to expect.

'My wife is a Muslim,' I told him at one point, hoping to impress, not

125

mentioning that she was of the vodka-swilling Eurasian version of Islam and had never been in a mosque in her life. Of course, for Sheikh Hamad that meant she was an apostate, but I didn't know that at the time.

In the end it didn't make a difference; it seemed they'd done their research and had already made their minds up. Much more experienced senior broadcast executives were in the frame, but again I had been coached on how to pitch my vision of the new channel and my proposed fees, which were significantly below any of the other candidates. Within the hour the deal was sealed, and Mahmoud congratulated me as we stepped back into the searing heat, then drove me back to the Ritz-Carlton for several large whiskies to celebrate.

'I got the job, can you believe it?' I told Zoulfia when I called her. 'I can't believe it; we're moving to Doha.'

'When?' She was excited too, fed up with life in south London.

'Sooner than you think. I'll see you back in London.'

Within a month we were all flown back to Qatar, again in first class, for a couple of weeks to begin drawing up the first draft of operational plans.

The story of the eventual successful launch of Al Jazeera English has been well documented, so I won't repeat it here, although the tensions between the staff of the Arabic channel and their new noisy neighbours are less well known.

Mostly it seemed to be a mixture of distrust and jealousy. Distrust because they feared we would dilute the Al Jazeera brand, with its fiery support for the Palestinian cause, Hamas in the Gaza strip and the Muslim Brotherhood in Egypt in particular. Jealousy because of all the publicity we were receiving in the Western media, and the fact that we were being paid more. There was no way we could attract big-name Western broadcasters on the kind of money being paid to the Egyptians and Palestinians who made up the bulk of the Arabic channel's staff. We had visits from President Mubarak of Egypt, Hugo Chávez of Venezuela, Israel's Shimon Peres with his dead fish eyes, and a host of other world leaders and politicians, including from the UK. None of them were very impressive; in the flesh they were just so ordinary, and I used to wonder how they came to be in the positions they occupied.

'What? So much trouble from this matchbox?' Mubarak exclaimed when he saw how small the Al Jazeera compound was.

'You are the warriors of truth!' Chavez proclaimed.

My counterpart at the Arabic channel, Wadah, a Palestinian in his late thirties, overweight and clean-shaven with thinning hair, and a staunch Hamas supporter, did everything in his power, it seemed to me, to delay the launch of the English channel. When that failed and we duly launched, he changed tactics, and the cull of our senior management began.

First to go was Paul Gibbs, our director of programmes, a perennially cheerful figure despite serious health problems. I was on holiday with my family when Wadah moved on him. Paul made the mistake of telling Wadah he would have to 'consider his position' if Wadah kept interfering, and Wadah gleefully took that as an offer to resign.

Paul was escorted from his office and made to walk in temperatures hitting forty degrees Celsius to Television Roundabout just outside the compound, where he flagged down a taxi. Never mind that nearly all the programmes still running on Al Jazeera English were Paul's ideas; I felt Wadah was only interested in his own personal vendetta.

When I returned to Doha I went ballistic, especially about the way Paul had been made to walk in the sweltering heat despite his ill health. 'If he had to be fired, that's my job, not yours! But there was no reason to fire him anyway, and now I'm guessing he'll sue you under UK law, because he was hired to the London office, not Doha. What were you thinking, making him walk to the roundabout?'

'That's not the Al Jazeera way.' Wadah actually seemed slightly embarrassed.

'Well, it's what happened, so what are you going to do about it?'

There was no way Paul could be reinstated, there was too much *face* involved for that, it was a done deed, but he did at least get generous compensation.

Next up was our director of finance, Gary Napier, a tall, square-jawed and imposing man who'd made the mistake of making his counterparts at the Arabic channel look incompetent, which wasn't very hard.

'Fuck me,' Gary said as he packed his bags. 'I came here as a liberal and I'm leaving as a raving right-winger; these people are beyond contempt.'

I was the last, my cardinal sin being to refuse to allow Sheikh Hamad to impose another Egyptian on our newsroom as an 'advisor' on editorial direction. I don't remember his name; we met briefly in the Doha Sheraton and it was enough to convince me that he was not for us. He was a chain-smoking rat-faced man who worked for the rival Saudi-backed Al Arabiya channel in Dubai, whose journalists told us confidentially that he was deeply unpopular and that they'd be glad to see the back of him. They got their wish shortly after I was ejected with a healthy compensation package.

In all we'd been in Doha for five years, five years during which the Manouche had barely featured in my thoughts apart from thumbing through old photographs. Zoulfia and I retain many fond memories of our time spent there, despite the politics, and the channel is a huge success, but all good things come to an end. I never got any thanks from Sheikh Hamad; he didn't even say goodbye.

On the upside, apart from the generous tax-free salary for five years and the exit package, we'd also made back all the money we'd lost in Spain after investing in an off-plan apartment block in Doha which we sold just days before the crash of 2008. I'd insisted on cash, and had returned home with plastic shopping bags stuffed with almost two million riyals.

Africa

Back in London yet again but flush with money this time, we bought a modest semi-detached house close to our former flat, which we had gifted to Daniel and Simon, and Zoulfia's son by her first marriage, Sasha. I wrote to Beudjeu but received no reply, and pondered a holiday in France to revisit the Manouche. I thought I'd never work again; I mean, how many people were stupid or vain enough to sink millions into a news channel which would probably never see a profit, unless it was government-funded and for propaganda? But I was wrong.

Lindsey Oliver, who'd been in charge of distribution at Al Jazeera English, called me one day. I was very fond of her even if she was as mad as a box of frogs, and we'd become good friends.

'Fancy a trip to Nigeria?' she asked.

'Nigeria? You're kidding, right?'

'No, I'm deadly serious. There are plans for a new pan-African news channel. Shall I put your name forward?'

'Why not? Africa is the only continent I've not lived and worked in; that would make it a full house!'

'By the way,' she added before ringing off, 'I got a new car.'

'Yeah? What is it?'

'It's blue,' she said.

'Yes, but what make?'

'I don't know; all I know is that it's blue,' she said. That was Lindsey.

I went to a meeting in a London hotel with a shady but charming man called Toyin who outlined the plans for the new channel, which would be based in Lagos. He invited me out to meet the man who was behind the venture, a billionaire called Bola Tinubu who owned the biggest chain of petrol stations in the country. Tinubu was obsessed with politics, and would become the driving force behind the 2015 election of President Muhammadu Buhari, whose new party, the APC, swept aside the incumbent president Goodluck Jonathan and the ruling PDP party which had been in power since 1999. The APC's party symbol was a broom and they promised a clean sweep to wipe out corruption and end the Boko Haram insurgency, even though in the event nothing actually changed. It was 2011, and Bola clearly saw a pan-African news channel as an ideal vehicle for furthering his political ambitions.

Nigeria's reputation went before it. I'd been to Kenya and South Africa on holidays, but Nigeria was the big beast of the continent and I was wary. The sum total of my knowledge of the country was that, like so many people, I often received emails promising instant wealth if I would only let a Nigerian prince use my bank account to park millions of dollars for a short time, and that it was neck and neck with Russia as one of the most corrupt countries in the world.

I was not reassured when I arrived at London's Heathrow airport to check in with British Airways, only to find there was no ticket. I called Toyin, who was supposed to meet me, to discover he had already checked in and was enjoying his breakfast in the business-class lounge.

'Don't worry, I'll sort it,' he said cheerfully.

I was nonplussed, but within twenty minutes, as I hovered by the check-in desks, an e-ticket duly arrived and I went through to join Toyin. I was to learn that this was fairly typical of Nigeria; things tended to work out in the end, but it wasn't always clear how.

It was June, the rainiest month of the long rainy season; the mildew even seemed to be creeping up the walls of my supposedly five-star hotel on Victoria Island, although the only five-star aspect of the place was the price, and the traffic was horrendous. Lagos is a teeming anthill of 20 million people or more; nobody knows for sure. Every day thousands more arrive from the country, drawn like metal filings to the magnet of promised wealth: a city of hustlers and big business, movies from 'Nollywood', which churns out more films every year than Hollywood, and the thrum of *Naija* music.

'Three things you need to know about Nigeria,' Toyin said with a grin before we met Bola. 'We are the most religious, the most corrupt and the happiest people on earth.'

Well, I wasn't sure about the last one, but the people were certainly exuberant and it wasn't long before I fell in love with them. Unexpectedly Lagos also felt safe in a way that, for example, Johannesburg didn't. Sure, they would rob you blind given half a chance, but violence against foreigners was rare. In Johannesburg it was more of a case of 'You got no money, man? Okay, we'll shoot you anyway.' That didn't happen in Lagos, even if the north of the country, where a bloody Islamic insurgency was raging, was a no-go area.

Bola himself was a small man in traditional robes, a Muslim married to a Christian, which was not so unusual in Lagos. His head was clean-shaven, like a lot of the Lagosians, and he laughed when I asked if they all went to the same barber. His eyes glinted with sharp intelligence, and he loved London; he kept an apartment just off Regent's Park, which he visited regularly in his private jet. We immediately struck up a bond, and it was that more than anything that convinced me to take on this madcap venture.

We went to visit his television compound on the mainland, where he already operated a local channel, TVC, and a radio station, RC. The buildings were run down and smelled of damp, white egrets picked their way around the rubbish, and there was a building site which was to be the headquarters of the new international TVC, but nothing much seemed to be happening there. It was all a bit depressing and there seemed to be a mountain to climb to get this project off the ground.

Nevertheless we agreed terms and on the last evening Toyin took me to meet some of the other players in a French-themed bistro in Ikoyi. There I met Lemi Olalemi (the then head of TVC, a tall, softly spoken and intelligent man who had suffered imprisonment under the military dictatorships before escaping to operate a pirate radio station out of Norway), Richard Dayo Johnson (who headed the radio station, a larger-than-life character with such a posh English accent that if you only spoke to him on the telephone you'd imagine he was an old

Etonian) and Sanjay Salil (the owner of MediaGuru from India, who would be installing all our technical equipment).

'You better get going,' Lemi said when it was still only five thirty in the evening and I was halfway through my steak and chips.

'But the flight isn't for another five hours.'

'Trust me, when it's raining like this the traffic can be bad.'

That was an understatement. We crawled across the Third Mainland Bridge, which Nigerians like to boast is Africa's longest bridge although it's really a causeway, and kept crawling all the way to the airport, arriving more than three hours later and just in time to get through the chaotic check-in and immigration procedures. Without the rain and Friday-night traffic it should have been a drive of thirty to forty minutes.

Again the Manouche faded into the background as I spent the next five years commuting between London and Lagos, two weeks out and one week at home. We decided not to move out as a family because Nikita was coming up to secondary school and we felt she needed the chance to put down some roots.

I was joined in Lagos by a former colleague from Al Jazeera English, Stuart Young, who became TVC's director of news. He did move there full-time with his wife Jane and their two young twin daughters, my goddaughters, Katherine and Natasha.

In many ways the project was more fulfilling than Al Jazeera because we literally had to train up all the journalists. We couldn't hire from existing channels and especially not from the state-sponsored ones, simply because they had too many ingrained bad habits, not least that of expecting payment from companies or individuals in return for favourable reports. They would never give us the kind of hard-hitting and unbiased reporting we were after. But the Nigerians are nothing if not enthusiastic and fast learners, and as the months slid by and the building slowly took shape, so did the team. They were also incredibly patient and always polite; apart from myself I never heard anyone swear in all the time I spent in Lagos.

Another thing I loved about Nigeria was the total lack of any kind of political correctness.

'Hey, whitey!' people would regularly shout to me, waving and smiling as Rotimi, my driver, negotiated his way through the traffic. 'What you doing here?'

I would wave back; there was nothing malicious in it, and I remembered doing the same in London back in the 1960s when I saw Africans or Caribbean people there for the first time, something that would be unimaginable today.

'Hey, look, a white African!' Rotimi said another day with a laugh, pointing at an albino pushing a wheelbarrow of yams in the street, and again he meant no harm. Life is hard in Lagos; there are no safety nets and people deal with it with dark humour.

We opened small offices in Johannesburg, Nairobi, Cairo and London and duly launched early in 2013 with the slogan *Through African Eyes*. A few months later TVC began airing on BSkyB in the UK and picked up several international awards. It was a good channel, offering programmes on health and women's issues, travel and debates, along with its regular news bulletins. But, whereas Al Jazeera had fed off the pan-Arabic identity across the Middle East, we soon learned there was no equivalent pan-African identity. People in Nigeria were simply not interested, for example, in what was happening in Mozambique or Zimbabwe, and vice versa. If anything, they were more interested in events in the United States or the UK.

Bola also soon realised that the costly pan-African model did little to further his domestic political ambitions, and within a couple of years decided to close all the international bureaux except for London. TVC became a Nigeria-centric channel, which held little appeal for me. All the fun had been in putting the channel together and getting on air, so in late 2016 I tendered my resignation and returned once more to London, and this time it really was to retire.

A Lightbulb Moment

R etirement is something many people dream of, but after a lifetime of work I found it difficult to adjust without any structure to my days. For a year I did almost nothing except read incessantly, play the occasional game of golf, go to the gym, drink too much, and get depressed. One of the problems was that none of my friends could afford to retire, so shared activities were almost impossible.

'Does anyone retire any more?' Eddy asked. 'I can't afford to. I think I'll just have to work until I drop.' He was twice expensively divorced and now running his own landscape gardening business.

Meanwhile Nikita was enjoying school, breezing through exams and becoming increasingly independent, so Zoulfia and I were redundant in more ways than one.

During one of those interminably dark London winter days when the sky seems about two inches above your head and the rain looks like it will never stop, we decided to finally try to sort through the thousands of photographs we'd amassed over the years, and it wasn't long before I stumbled across my old pictures of the Manouche. It had been nearly thirty years since I'd seen them, twenty-seven to be precise, and I had been forty years old then, but looking through those old photographs I realised I'd rarely been happier than during my days with them. Suddenly I knew what I had to do, and after hours rooting through dozens of boxes in the garage, I found my old notes of my time in the caravans and began to write this account.

It was a struggle; nothing seemed to come together, and every time I reread my efforts even I could see it was boring.

'It's unreadable!' Gary, my former comrade-in-arms from Al Jazeera days, told me from his poolside in New Zealand, in his usual blunt manner which had failed so spectacularly to endear him to the Arabs.

The trouble was that I seemed to write as a journalist, which was hardly surprising, boiling everything down to the bare bones and barely using adjectives. In the end, full of trepidation and doubts, I took myself off to a writer's retreat buried in the depths of Shropshire, where a small group of us were mentored by published writers. There was no internet, no television, no mobile signal and no radio, and to say it was intense would be an understatement. But it was also a revelation, as if a blindfold had been removed, I learned to enjoy writing for the sake of it again, it became a joy instead of a chore, and I started rewriting *Manouche* from the beginning.

'Bloody hell, it's a great read,' Gary told me when I sent him the first 5,000 words of the new version. 'Send me the rest of it, I want to finish it!'

'No more until I get to the end,' I told him. 'If I keep sending it out in dribs and drabs I'm worried it'll be diluted, it'd be a distraction.'

'I always find it easiest to start at the end and work your way back,' my old friend Ed Mitchell from EBC days said as we shared a rare lunch together on the Brighton seafront shortly before Christmas 2018. He'd recently had a book published about his own fall from grace, decent into alcoholism and eventual recovery, entitled *From Headlines to Hard Times*.

'But I don't know what the ending is; how can I start there?'

'So you've no idea how this story will finish up at all?'

'Not really.'

'So, what, you're going to go on pootling along until it runs into the sand and just stops? There's got to be a proper ending!'

'You're right,' I said, pushing my spaghetti bolognese around and looking at him. 'And there's only one way to find out what that ending might be.'

It was a lightbulb moment; I knew I had to go back to Marseille and try to track down the Manouche again.

I had no van any more, but I did have a beautiful old black and pearl-white Triumph Bonneville T100 motorbike sitting in the garage, the last twin-carb model they made before introducing fuel injection

technology. With its pea shooter exhausts it sounded like a real motorbike from the sixties, but without the ubiquitous oil leaks of Triumphs
from that era. I'd barely used it for more than two years, mainly
because we'd acquired a small dog called Brandy who needed walking
every day, a cross between a Cavalier King Charles and a bichon frise,
and dogs and motorbikes don't really go together.

Taking the bike in winter was to prove to be a mad decision, but it
seemed a good idea at the time. I thought it would give me freedom, it
would be cheaper than the car, and anyway it'd been a long time since
I'd enjoyed a proper long-distance bike tour. Zoulfia said I should take
an aeroplane and just hire a car at the other end, and as usual she was
right.

The bike was reluctant to start; the petrol in the tank had turned to
gunk. For some reason modern petrols degrade much quicker than the
old ones; at least that's what my mechanic told me. Maybe it's since
they took the lead out, but the tank had to be flushed and the carburet-
tors cleaned and the bike given a full service, the chain tightened and
tyres checked, before it was ready to go.

I had my old soft saddle bags and tank top, and bought a helmet box
for the rear rack. I thought about fitting a small windscreen; it would
have spoiled the classic look but would also mean a lot less buffeting
from the wind on the long ride back to the south of France, but in the
end I didn't bother. I'd spent enough, and anyway I liked the classic
look of the old Triumph.

I also treated myself to new winter motorcycle boots and gloves, plus
a new helmet after learning that my old one was at least five years past
its use-by date, and a fantastically warm all-weather riding suit, black
and white like the bike, with built-in protectors for the knees, elbows
and back. I stopped short of fitting heated handlebars.

Once more I packed spare jeans, thermal underwear, a few T-shirts
and a couple of pullovers, a small tent and sleeping bag, and a digital
camera. I'd also found boxes of my old 35mm slides from the early days
with the Manouche, and tracked down a specialist to print off a couple
of dozen prints from them which I hoped I could use to jog the memo-

ries of some of the younger members of the company from those days, on the assumption that many of the older ones such as Chocote and Oumlo had probably since passed away. My greatest hope was that at least Beudjeu, and his brothers Blon, Pepite and Niglo, would still be around, and that they were still living in the dockside houses they'd been moved into. If not, finding them or their descendants could be nigh on impossible.

By the end of January I was ready to go, but then the weather had a say. In London the temperature dropped sharply, below zero Celsius at night and only hovering around three or four degrees in the day, and it started sleeting. It was also snowing in France, even in the south just north of Marseille. After trying a couple of runs to Brighton and Portsmouth to get the feel of the bike again, I realised I had to wait until the temperatures rose. No matter how good my new all-weather gear was, my hands were frozen within half an hour and icy water dripped from my helmet down the back of my neck.

Don't get me wrong; I love motorbikes. For me they represent a special kind of freedom on a par maybe with riding a horse at full gallop along a deserted beach, and in nearly fifty years of biking I'd only had two crashes – one when I hit a kangaroo in Australia, which earned me a few days in hospital in a nowhere place called Paraburdoo after a couple of miners in a pick-up found me lying by the roadside, an accident for which I laid the blame firmly on the kangaroo, and the other in Reading, when a lorry driver inexplicably pulled out to turn right just in front of me, which meant I dropped off the bike to slide across the road while watching my first ever Triumph Bonneville get written off under the wheels of the truck. But even so, riding in wintery sleet with poor visibility is not a lot of fun.

It was an anxious time as I'd decided that, come what may, I needed to make the trip before the Manouche travelling season of old kicked off, on the off-chance that they did still actually leave to go travelling in the spring. If they did, and I missed them in Marseille, finding them would pretty much be a lost cause. I was also thinking of the alleged Brexit deadline of 29th March, when the UK was due to leave the

European Union, and the possible extra issues that could raise, such as maybe needing a visa and no longer having a valid European Health Insurance card. Checking the long-range weather forecasts became a daily obsession, but as January drifted into February the outlook remained grim.

The other thing that was bothering me was reports that the French were actively getting rid of the Manouche and other Gypsies. The French authorities had sent more than 10,000 Romanies back to Bulgaria and Romania in 2009,[1] and in 2010 and 2011 had organised 'repatriation' flights to send French Gypsies to Romania, bribing them with € 300 per adult and € 100 per child.[2] Which all seemed perverse while they were admitting tens of thousands of migrants from sub-Saharan Africa.

Some 8,000 Gypsies were sent to Romania in 2011 and forced to sign papers saying they would never return to France.[3] I wondered if my former friends and family could have possibly been among them. It was alleged that the French were targeting Gypsy communities living in the cities, but the websites I had found were thin on detail. I decided that it was unlikely that my company had been targeted, and doubted very much they would have got on an aeroplane to a foreign country for the pittance offered. Surely they had attained official French identity papers when they had been moved into their purpose-built houses, after all? The trip would go ahead, sooner or later. And my gear stayed packed, sitting on the kitchen floor in the saddle bags.

---

[1]   Suddath, Claire. 'Who are gypsies, and why is France deporting them?' *Time*, 26 Aug. 2010

[2]   Czech Press Agency. 'France resumes deportations of Roma people from Romania'. Romea.cz, 13 Apr. 2011

[3]   Czech Press Agency. 'France resumes deportations of Roma people from Romania'. Romea.cz, 13 Apr. 2011

The Return

I finally set off on 27th February 2019, after a week of unseasonably warm weather which saw the temperature in London hitting twenty degrees Celsius, but the gods love to laugh at us and maybe I should have known better.

I stopped overnight with friends in the old Saxon village of Stelling Minnis twenty miles north of Dover but barely slept because of excitement, then set off at dawn on what promised to be another fine day to catch an early ferry. I was the only biker on the boat.

'How come?' I asked one of the deckhands who was helping me lash the Triumph securely in place.

'Because you're the only one stupid enough to go biking at this time of the year!' he laughed. Prophetic words.

All the memories of those old crossings to see my Manouche family came rushing back as I stood on deck watching the grey waters of the English Channel churn by and the white cliffs of Dover disappear into the mist. In no time we were docking in Calais and Sod's law kicked in as I emerged to grey skies and the first spits of rain.

I decided to take the motorway and try to reach Lyon that first day, a distance of around 400 miles which would kill the journey. French motorways are good but expensive, even if the rate for a motorbike is a lot less than for a car. But within a hundred miles the rain was chucking it down; I was soon soaked and kept being buffeted by huge trucks from Lithuania, Poland, the Netherlands and Romania. Every time I passed one the wind was snatched away and I swayed across my lane and felt vulnerable. For a while I tucked in behind an Eddie Stobart truck; it sounds absurd and probably is, but somehow I felt comforted that I was getting spray from an English truck instead of those East European behemoths.

Northern France is a bleak and dreary landscape with few trees to break the violent wind; it's no wonder there are so many of those ugly electricity windmills like giant aliens marching across the flat fields. No wonder also that the Normans were such tough bastards, or that they opted to leave such an unforgiving place and invade England's lush south with its soft rolling hills instead. Poor Harold and the lads probably didn't stand a chance. Those were the kinds of thoughts that flashed through my brain as I struggled to stay focussed in the foul weather, passing signposts announcing Picardy, the Marne, Verdun, the Ardennes, names that evoked battles from Agincourt to the World Wars. If those poor young soldiers could survive the mud and gore of those places, surely my lot wasn't so bad – even if they didn't have to put up with a windchill factor which came from bombing along at 70 miles per hour and more.

I found myself having to stop every hour just to warm up; my hands especially were freezing and the water had found its way inside my allegedly waterproof trousers to drench my thermal leggings until I was just sitting in a puddle. The Triumph also needed regular filling; it had a fairly small tank and no fuel indicator. I knew its maximum reach on a full tank was about 120 or 130 miles but always stopped well in advance of that, paranoid that I could run out of petrol and end up on the hard shoulder of the motorway in teeming rain.

The grey skies brought an early dusk and Lyon was looking unlikely, and then impossible when I pulled over one more time to refill the Triumph's tank. When I went to restart it, the bike's alarm went off and wouldn't stop, I couldn't turn it off with the key fob as usual, which meant I couldn't get the engine going either; the system was all interlinked. A man emerged from the station's shop and told me that the nearby telephone mast was interfering with the alarm system.

'It happens all the time,' he said. 'Especially with Harleys.'

He kindly helped me push the bike a couple of hundred yards behind some trees, which he said would block the telephone mast's signals, and sure enough after ten minutes or so the bike fired up again.

'Best stay off the motorways,' my rescuer said.

It seemed weird to me; if it was such a problem, why did they position the masts in the service stations in the first place? Clearly the president didn't ride a bike, I thought as I gunned on further down the motorway, stopping once more to fill up without incident before pulling into the small town of Chaumont, still a hundred miles or more north of Lyon.

In the old cobbled centre an Ibis hotel blinked a welcome. Thankfully they had a room to spare, and more importantly an underground garage where I could safely park up and unload my saddle bags. Everything inside was damp, and I draped my things around the room to dry out before heading out to a charming and bustling traditional French restaurant twenty yards away, ordering a plate of veal kidneys and a half-litre pitcher of red wine. Then I slept the deep and dreamless sleep of the dead.

My alarm woke me with a start just after seven and for a moment I didn't know where I was. My arms ached, my back ached, then I looked around at my scattered belongings and knew I had no choice but to hit the road again. I peeked out of the window; the sky was still slate grey, but it wasn't raining, and I felt relieved and ready for the road ahead as I headed down to breakfast. Halfway through my second double espresso accompanied by a ham baguette, though, I looked out of the window again and the rain was tipping down once more. My spirits sank.

I briefly toyed with the idea of staying another day and night in my very comfortable room, but the forecast for the next few days wasn't promising and I knew I'd only be putting off the inevitable. I delayed anyway, hoping the deluge might ease, and searched for the Manouche houses in Marseille on Google Earth – and found nothing.

'Fuck it,' I said to myself. 'I should have just taken the plane and hired a car like Zoulfia said.' Yes, I had started talking to myself. I felt that the whole trip was turning into a fool's errand. I called Zoulfia, ready to pour out my misery, only to find out she'd broken a bone in her foot doing some yoga exercise.

'Shall I turn back?' I asked almost in hope.

'No, don't be daft, you're halfway there, you have to see it through. I'll be fine.'

So that escape was blocked, and anyway she was right; this was no time to cop out, I felt like slapping myself. In fact I think I did. Then I lugged my baggage back down to the garage and tied it all in place and eased out into the pouring rain and went back onto the motorway to Lyon.

I kept stopping again every hour or so just to try to dry out a bit and warm up, but at the second stop the alarm went crazy again and this time I called roadside rescue. Fortunately I was covered by insurance; unfortunately they told me that as I was on a motorway they would only cover me for £60.

'It's on page 5 in the small print of your policy,' the man at rescue-mycar.com told me, not very helpfully.

'Who gets to page 5 of the small print?' I asked wearily.

'It's your responsibility to read it all carefully,' I was told.

There was no answer to that, so I waited for the rescue truck, which turned up within the hour and took me and the bike to a garage a couple of miles away. There the head mechanic *oof*ed and *pouff*ed and said 'oh la la' a few times in the French way before gleefully relieving me of €120. Well, it wasn't so bad, and when they put the bike into the garage it immediately started again.

'I know what it is,' said the mechanic.

'Don't tell me; it's the phone masts?'

'*Ah, oui, c'est ca, exactement!*' he said. 'It happens a lot, especially to Harleys, though it's the first time I've seen it with a Triumph.'

'Yeah, I've heard it.' I was starting to hate France.

I carried on. Lyon wasn't so far, but I needed one more stop for petrol, and of course the alarm started off again. This time I wheeled the bike myself a good quarter of a mile and hid behind some trucks to block the alleged signals from the phone masts. And, hey presto, it worked again!

Then I realised I'd lost my passport and credit card; whilst wheeling the bike I hadn't zipped up my pockets and they must have fallen out. I walked back to the service station and as I looked around inside, panicking, the woman at the till immediately asked me, 'Are you looking for something? A credit card, perhaps?'

'Yes, it ends in 6008, have you got it?'

'I need some ID.'

I showed her my driving licence. She produced the card and gave it back; apparently an honest Dutchman had handed it in.

'What about a passport?' I asked. 'I've lost that too.'

'*Rien.*' She shook her head. 'Maybe have a look outside?'

I went out, back into the rain, and unbelievably there was my passport lying in a puddle on the forecourt. For a moment, and for the first time, I really felt there was maybe someone looking out for me after all. I was bedraggled, depressed for sure, but losing the passport and credit card would have been the kiss of death. Suddenly my spirits lifted and my heartbeat calmed and I no longer felt that the world was against me.

I pulled off the motorway at the northern outskirts of Lyon on a whim – I can't remember the name of the suburb, even; I had just had enough of riding in the wet – but as soon as I did, there like a beacon was the green Ibis Budget sign. It seemed like a good omen and I pulled up in front of reception and asked for a room. They had just one single room left: perfect, and it was cheap, even if was soon obvious why.

The place seemed to be modelled on an American motel, a single-storey building in a U-shape with little rooms and a parking place in front of each. It was spartan but it was warm, and I quickly unloaded the saddle bags again and spread all my gear across the radiators, which I turned up to the maximum before covering the bike and taking a scalding hot shower. The only restaurant around was a pizzeria a hundred yards down the road, but I didn't care. Lyon might be the culinary capital of France, but right then a pizza and a bottle of red seemed like manna from heaven, and within an hour of guzzling them I was fast asleep again.

The next day, after a rushed breakfast of the usual double espressos and baguette in a crowded restaurant area (the place was crammed with Dutch and German tourists with expensive Audis, Mercedes,

BMWs and Volvos, which was a mystery to me; surely they could afford somewhere better?), I headed off once again. By the time I got to the other side of Lyon signs for Marseille had already started appearing even though it was still more than 200 miles away, and this time I opted for the scenic route, staying well clear of the motorways and their dreaded phone masts.

It was a beautiful ride on small winding roads up into the hills south of Lyon and down the other side, a biker's dream road. Even a light drizzle at the top of the hills did little to dampen my spirits. I could see the sky was lighter to the south and knew the rain would soon pass, and anyway at the slower speed it wasn't cold and didn't penetrate my clothing.

Other bikers appeared; I realised I hadn't seen a single one north of Lyon, but now they appeared in increasing numbers, sometimes singly, more often in packs. Those coming towards me all waved a greeting which gave me a warm feeling, like belonging to a fraternity of some kind. Those overtaking would suddenly stuck their right boot out, which confused me at first – the only time you see bikers sticking a boot out like that in London is when they're trying to kick a taxi or something – but after the first half-dozen I realised this was also their way of greeting me. In general the French are much more bike-friendly than the English, maybe because for many of them it is a summer pastime rather than a life choice, so the majority of French bikers also drive cars, which is not always the case in England.

The other thing that struck me was the number of McDonald's restaurants everywhere. There seemed to be as many of them as petrol stations; every small town had at least one, even if their livery was green, maybe a French legal requirement to tone down the brash American red and yellow colours which are their norm. Not only that, but when I pulled into one for lunch, it had table service – it really was McDonald's *à la française* – and it was packed. The French had clearly taken to the fast-food outlet with a passion, and the cheeseburger with fries and coffee was probably the best lunch I'd had on the trip so far.

I passed through sleepy decrepit villages in which half the houses seemed to be abandoned while the others all had their window shutters closed. In most of them there wasn't a soul to be seen, and I wondered what people did for entertainment in places like that. Not a lot, at a guess, and the idea of living in one of those sad little villages held little attraction.

Then I was out on the main roads again, the *routes nationales* which are the equivalent of the UK's A roads, past Valence, then Orange and finally Avignon. A lot of the roundabouts had little guillotines on them with effigies in yellow jackets and slogans denouncing President Macron, a reflection of the weeks of protests the country had been witnessing against his economic policies, which were seen to favour the rich at the expense of ordinary men and women.

It was still early afternoon, so I decided to push on for the last sixty-odd miles to Marseille. During that last stretch every possible permutation of my journey's end kept flashing through my mind. Would the Gypsies still be there and, if so, would I be able to find them? Would they remember me? Who might still be alive and who would have passed away? What if those little houses had been demolished and the Gypsies rehoused somewhere entirely different? Why had I embarked on this madcap venture in the first place?

Then as I crested a rise I saw the city sprawled out below and the huge sign of Marseille spelled out in white letters on the hillside, a bit like the more famous Hollywood sign. I wasn't sure where to go and descended past bleak housing estates covered in graffiti, until before I knew it I was in the centre and close to the old port. I knew that was wrong, that I needed to be closer to the docks, so I turned around, and then I was like a homing pigeon.

I saw a sign for L'Estaque, which vaguely rang a bell, and followed it, stopping at a petrol station just short of the satellite town on the western side of Marseille. I asked a man about the Manouche, and showed him a photo of the little houses where Chocote and the others had been moved to so many years before.

'Yes, there are still Gypsies near here, you've gone past them. Go back and at the third roundabout turn left and come back again, and you'll see them on the right-hand side.'

'Is there a hotel near here?'

'Yes,' he said again. 'Turn right at the next roundabout and it's just up the hill.'

I thanked him profusely and headed back the way I'd come, following his directions. On the first pass I missed them and was soon back at the petrol station, so I tried once more. The giveaway was a wrecked white Renault van by the roadside; next to it I realised there was a narrow entrance to the few remaining resettlement houses, along with a variety of vans and caravans.

The place was hardly recognisable; the red houses that had once stood in neat rows were now bleached white and crumbling, with broken windows and doors. There were less than half of them left and it didn't look inviting.

I rode in cautiously, attracting curious stares, and stopped by a group of men drinking from cans of beer, but didn't turn the engine off. I looked over to Chocote's old house. It was falling apart, the *Place du Niglo* sign had disappeared and Oumlo's lovingly tended garden was long gone. I wanted to take a photograph of it but didn't feel comfortable surrounded by these strangers.

'Are you Manouche?' I asked.

'We are; what do you want?' one replied. They were all red-eyed but didn't seem aggressive, just puzzled by this foreigner on a bike riding into their camp.

'I used to live here. I'm looking for some friends,' I explained, and I pulled out my photos again, reeling off the names of Chocote and Oumlo, Beudjeu, Blon, Paquili, Koki and Pantoon.

'Pantoon is here! Up the hill,' the same man said. 'But the others are all gone.'

That didn't sound great, but Pantoon would be a start. They gave me directions to another resettlement estate about a mile away, and ten minutes later I was riding into another cluster of the same kind of houses, only obviously newer. There were numerous caravans dotted about. This time I stopped by a group of youths, several of them on mopeds, and the smell of marijuana was noticeable. Again I produced the photographs, which were passed around excitedly, and a young girl reached over to cut my engine. I wasn't feeling so confident or comfortable any more, until an old lady drew close.

'Chocote was my relative,' she said. 'I remember you.'

'And Meme was my grandfather,' said a youth in dark glasses astride a moped as he found a black-and-white photo of the man from our first *vendange*.

'What's your name?' I asked.

'Josef.'

'Where can I find Pantoon?'

'Follow me, I'll show you,' he said as I took the photos back. He took me one road further down and stopped outside a battered caravan, with flat tyres and windows held together with sticking tape, and banged on the door. Loud music was playing inside.

'Pantoon, there's a *gadjo* here to see you,' Josef called out.

'I'm not a *gadjo*,' I protested, but then I realised I probably was to him.

The music was cut, and a small sunburned man with a bald pate came outside. Gone were the long black locks and cheeky grin of the Pantoon of the past, but he was instantly recognisable just by his stance.

'You don't remember me, do you?' I said.

'No, who are you?'

'Nadjo. I used to live with Chocote and Oumlo and we worked the *vendanges* together.'

'Nadjo! Is it really you? Yes, it is, I can see it now, I remember, we still talk about you!' And he came forwards and embraced me, kissing both cheeks.

We sat in the sun outside his caravan looking through the photos, drinking coffee and smoking, while unbeknownst to me on the other side of the caravan disaster was unfolding.

'Who is that?' Pantoon passed one photo over.

'It's you!'

'So it is. Oh, how I've changed; those were good days. Remember the *vendanges*? They were the best days.'

I asked after all of the others. Chocote and Oumlo and Mochi had passed away; so had Paquili's second wife Nina and young Pepite, both taken by cancer. And young Volka.

'She was ill,' Pantoon said, but he didn't know what with, nor did he know what had happened to her husband, Matzo.

The others, Beudjeu, Blon, Niglo, Koki and Paquili, had all moved close to Limoges, a good 400 miles away. And Ghuno was with them too, apparently. I guessed she must have been nearing eighty years old.

'We can call them,' Pantoon said, and dialled Beudjeu's number, but there was no reply.

'We'll try again tomorrow,' I said. Dusk was falling and I needed to book into that hotel. I had thought I might stay with Beudjeu, but that was no longer an option.

Walking back around the caravan, my heart stopped. My saddle bags were open and my things lying on the ground. For several seconds my brain froze, I couldn't believe what I was seeing, or at least I couldn't process it, then I frantically searched inside the saddle bags and sure enough my laptop and camera had disappeared.

'Pantoon, come quick!' I called, filled with despair. The camera was not an expensive one, and the laptop was ten years old, but it had this book in it and countless photographs which I didn't want to lose. I felt a rising sense of panic and despair. Again this trip seemed to be cursed.

Pantoon quickly went up to the houses in the road above but soon returned looking despondent.

'It was kids,' he said. 'Drug addicts. There's no respect any more; all the kids are taking drugs.'

'You know who took my stuff, then?'

'Yes, I found them, but they've already sold it to buy drugs. I said we'd buy it back, but I don't know who has it. Maybe tomorrow we can get it back.'

'At least the laptop,' I said. 'I can live without the camera.' But I didn't have much hope.

We agreed to meet again the next morning and start the search, and I put what was left of my belongings back into the saddle bags and rode bitterly back to look for the hotel I'd been told about, which almost inevitably was another Ibis Budget.

After a meal in L'Estaque of steak tartare washed down with a bottle of local red I slept badly that night, waking regularly, still not believing what had happened, cursing myself in frustration for being so careless. Of course I was just another *gadjo* to those kids, there for the taking, just like the guy with his Simca outside Mirabeau. How could I be so dumb? I hadn't even put the alarm on the bike, thinking I was still 'family'. What an idiot.

Lele

The next morning I felt drained, but there was nothing to do but carry on. After my now customary French breakfast of baguette and honey washed down by a couple of double espressos, I left my baggage at the hotel and went back to Pantoon's caravan. At least the sky was clear and blue.

Pantoon was shamefaced, wearing the same grey pullover and track-suit bottoms as the day before; he looked like he'd slept in them.

'There's nothing,' he said, which was hardly a surprise. 'We need to wait.'

Josef turned up on his moped and said he was sure he could track the missing laptop down.

'If we have to buy it back I'll pay myself,' he boasted.

I told him I wanted to be on my way by midday and asked him to come back with news one way or another by then, and he promised he would. That was the last I saw of him.

Pantoon and I drank coffee and smoked roll-ups, and were soon joined by Lolo and Antoine, who'd been youngsters when I'd last been in Marseille. Others came, drawn to look through the photos, and one of those who came was old Julien in a wheelchair. He was a cousin of Chocote's, although he'd not joined us on the harvests. He kissed me on both cheeks and his eyes welled with tears as he looked at the old pictures, repeatedly kissing an image of Chocote and Oumlo posing with their wedding photograph.

'Don't you travel any more at all?' I asked Pantoon as he made me a salami sandwich.

'Not at all. Not even to Les Saintes; these days there are more *gadjos* there than Manouche. Nothing is the same. Everything has been taken from us.'

'I still go every year,' said a rheumy-eyed man who I didn't know, but who had joined us to look at the photographs. 'But Pantoon is right; there are more French and other *gadjos* from all over than Manouche there now. It's been stolen from us.'

'Like everything,' I muttered, 'including your culture and lifestyle.'

'What did you say?'

I repeated my comment, only louder this time.

'You're right,' said the man. 'Everything has been taken. Who are we now?'

'How about the guitar?' I turned back to Pantoon. 'Do you still play?'

'I still have it, but I don't play much any more. No one does. People just watch television, and there's no fires allowed.'

He looked sad and rumpled and his caravan was untidy and not very clean, not like the gleaming ones of old. I asked where his wife was.

'Gone,' he said without elaborating, and I didn't feel like probing any further.

Later I learned that five years earlier Pantoon had been busking in the centre of Marseille when a drunken Russian tourist came and snatched his guitar and broke it over his head. An enraged relative of Pantoon's immediately went to steal a car, donned gloves and a bala-clava and sprayed a bar full of tourists with his Kalashnikov. Three Russians and an Italian died, apparently.

'He abandoned the car and they never caught him. There are more than thirty Kalashs in Mirabeau,' Beudjeu would tell me later, confirm-ing the story. 'Marseille is a bad place; it's why we left.'

Midday came and went with no sign of Josef, and still we sat and smoked. I was jittery and probably not good company. Pantoon made each of us more sandwiches and coffee as young kids cycled around on broken bicycles. One stopped to ask me to put the rusted chain back on his, which he was pushing around with his feet; none of them seemed to speak Manouche, only French. The site was a dismal place; a cloud of hopelessness hung over it. Chocote's gloomy predictions of what would happen to them from years before had come to fruition; they were an abandoned people, stuck at the bottom of the pile in a desolate part of town, with little or no meaning to their lives. Those young children weren't travellers any more.

'I need to go,' I said eventually when it was mid-afternoon.

'Wait, keep waiting,' Pantoon pleaded. 'Don't give up.'

So we waited some more in the shade of his caravan, but I had given up hope. We tried phoning Beudjeu again and this time Blon picked up the phone.

'We're all here near to Limoges, in Magnac-Laval; you have to come,' he said.

'I will, but maybe not this time. I'm tired,' I told him.

'Call later, speak to Beudjeu,' Blon said. 'We remember you and still talk about you. We hope to see you soon.'

'I promise,' I told him and rang off, and made a note of Beudjeu's number in my mobile.

Then Koki's and Tac-Tac's son Lele turned up. He'd been a small child back in the old days but was now shaven-headed and with tattoos on his arms, and he looked a tough, no-nonsense character.

'*Zinder, zinder*,' he kept muttering as he leafed through the old photographs.

'You know some kids stole my laptop?' I asked him.

He looked shocked. 'No, impossible. I'll get it back, I swear.' Then he came across a photograph of Tac-Tac standing with me in a field, Lele on her hip. 'Let me take this,' he said to Pantoon. 'I'll find the bastards.'

We went to the houses in the street above and Lele made straight for a whey-faced youth standing in a group, grabbing him by the throat and lifting until the boy's toes were barely touching the ground. 'You see this?' Lele demanded, brandishing the photograph. 'This man is like an uncle to me, a cousin, and you steal from him?'

'I didn't know, I didn't know!' the youth gasped. His eyes were popping, his arms had needle marks and his nose was red raw.

'Drugs!' Lele spat. 'Where's the stuff? I want it back, now!'

'I sold it, I don't know.'

'Who did you sell it to? I swear I'll kill you if you don't tell me.' Lele was shouting now, and the boy caved and told him everything.

'Wait with Pantoon,' Lele said to me, letting the kid drop. 'I'll be back in half an hour.'

'Lele is crazy,' Pantoon said as we waited. 'No one likes to argue with him.'

True to his word, Lele came back in less than the promised time. 'I know where they are, I've seen them. The computer is grey and the camera is a red Nikon, is that right?'

'Sounds right,' I told him. 'What now?'

'We have to buy them back, these people aren't family. I'm sorry. I would pay but I have no money.'

I didn't have many euros, so Lele jumped on the back of the Triumph, not bothering with a helmet, and directed me to the closest cash machine about a mile away, where I took out € 150. Back at Pantoon's caravan I handed the money over to Lele and he said he'd be back in fifteen to twenty minutes. And again he was as good as his word, running to the caravan with a plastic bag, and there were my laptop and camera. I couldn't believe it; all the tension of the day flooded out and I hugged Lele and Pantoon. Okay so I'd had to fork out € 150 for what was essentially mine anyway, but I still had to think of it as a good result.

At the same time I had a sneaky suspicion that it had all been a bit too easy for Lele. Things seemed to have changed when I told them about this book I was writing which was all in the laptop, and how I wanted to donate any profits to the Manouche if it ever got published. I half-wondered if Lele himself hadn't actually been the laptop's buyer. I shoved the thought aside as paranoia. In the end I really didn't care; I was just happy to have everything back.

I was too drained by then to think of getting back on the road, so after emotional farewells I went back to the hotel, picking up a hamburger and bottle of wine on the way, and checked in for another night, ready for an early start the next day. Before sleeping I tried calling Beudjeu again, but it went to voicemail, so I left a message telling him the missed call was my phone number. Half an hour later he called back, almost too excited to speak.

'It's really you?' he asked. 'You have to come and see us, we're near Limoges.'

'I know, Blon told me, but I'm just so tired, Beudjeu, and it's hundreds of kilometres more for me to get there. I'll go home now and come again soon.'

'You must, you must, we have a house here, it's much better than Marseille, everyone is waiting.'

'I'll be there. Let's talk again soon when I'm back in London.'

He rang off and I sat musing. I really couldn't face the extra trip on the bike in this kind of weather, but despite all the mishaps throughout the journey it seemed it had been worthwhile after all. Against all the odds, I'd done what I had set out to do, which felt like a real achievement.

Marseille 2019; (L-R) Pantoon, Lolo, Antoine and Lele

Beudjeu

I left early the next day, filtering through the heavy Marseille traffic and onto the motorway back to Avignon, where I reverted to the *routes nationales* again. While the ride from Calais had evoked memories of past battles, in the other direction it was like a tour of famous vineyards as I passed Châteauneuf-du-Pape (an old favourite of my father's), Meursault, Côte de Beaune, Nuits-Saint-Georges and Champagne, not necessarily in that order. There was no rain but the wind was gale force, there were red warning signs flashing and, as I pressed on past Lyon in the darkening gloom, each time a truck passed the other way it was like a full-body punch, my head rocking back and the bike swaying. Eventually, though, well after 8pm and after twelve hours on the road, the lights of Chaumont twinkled their welcome and I was soon checked into the same hotel as before, the bike stowed safely and dryly in the underground garage. I stripped off my stinking clothes, took a hot shower and headed downstairs for a beef bourguignon, then fell into another deep sleep after once more setting my alarm for an early start. I dreamed I was still on the road, the bike vibrating in my hands, the rain still falling and the wind still buffeting.

Sure enough, I awoke to the sound of heavy rain and peered disconsolately out of the window at yet another leaden sky. After breakfast I checked the forecast, thinking to stay another day in the warmth, but rain was predicted for the rest of the week, so I reluctantly picked my warm gloves, thermal long johns and socks off the radiators, got dressed and headed down to the garage with my gear.

It was the worst day riding of the trip yet. Now I knew why I was the only biker on the road, and by the time I reached Reims the rain had only got heavier. It battered my helmet as if someone were throwing frozen peas at me, and my feet, arse, legs and the rest of me were soon all soaked. I had intended on stopping another night before taking the ferry, but I was so wet anyway I decided to throw caution to the wind and head straight for Calais; it was only just past midday and the port wasn't more than 200 miles further. Again I risked the motorway, hurtling along at eighty miles per hour but stopping regularly to get some feeling back into my hands, although I didn't turn off the engine even when filling the tank or taking a toilet break in case the alarm did its thing again and I became stranded.

Approaching Calais, the motorway was reduced to a single lane for about twenty miles; the other lanes were full of trucks that had been backed up and parked because French customs were on strike, claiming they would have extra work if and when Brexit ever happened in the UK. I eventually reached the port by 4.30pm and went straight to the ticket office, parked and had no choice this time but to switch the engine off before I went in. And this time the bike really seemed to die; even the key fob showed no signs of life.

A snooty and unfriendly woman at the desk of one ferry company showed no interest in my plight and refused to sell me a ticket unless I could get the bike started. The next company along were much more sympathetic; they still couldn't sell me a ticket but said if I could start the engine I should go straight to check-in and get a ticket there. There was a ferry leaving in half an hour, and another one an hour and a half after that.

I went back outside, pushing the alarm fob again and again until my thumb hurt, but it was hopeless. I was at my wits' end. I couldn't see any phone masts but imagined there were a lot of signals in the port area and put it down to that. Then a local down-and-out approached me and asked for a cigarette, and I passed him my sodden pouch of Golden Virginia.

'What's the problem?' he asked as he sucked hard on his roll-up, trying to get the damp tobacco to light.

'The problem is I think I'm going to have to share a bench with you tonight,' I said. 'I can't get it started, the alarm keeps going off and now even the alarm fob isn't working; there's no light flashing like there should be. I don't know what to do.'

'Give me your keys,' he said. 'Have you got a screwdriver or something?'

I did, and, after rummaging in my saddle bags, handed it and the keys over. He quickly took the fob apart, then held a lighter under the batteries for a few minutes. All of a sudden the fob sprang back into life, and he quickly reassembled it and handed the keys back to me.

'You had water inside,' he said with a shrug.

'Fuck!' I exclaimed. All that gibberish about phone masts, even from the roadside rescue people, had been just that. Gibberish. That's why I'd had no problem in the sunshine of Marseille, only in the days of rain I'd been riding. Why couldn't I have worked that out? I guess basically because anything remotely technical or mechanical leaves me stumped. It had taken a tramp bumming a cigarette to sort it out. I could have hugged him but settled for handing him the rest of the tobacco as the bike fired up first time and I raced off to the check-in.

I'd missed the first ferry, but bought a ticket for the next one at 6.30 pm, then went to a waiting room where I again disassembled the key fob and warmed the batteries some more. I was paranoid that the key batteries would fail again and leave me stranded on the quayside.

Half an hour before the ferry was due to leave I went back outside and watched it dock. Well before the incoming trucks and cars had finished rolling off, I gingerly tried the ignition, and *voila*! It worked first time again, and I left the engine idling until it was time to board.

Once the bike was securely lashed in place I headed straight for the restaurant and ordered fish and chips with mushy peas and a hot chocolate. Apart from a bar of chocolate, I hadn't eaten since my breakfast baguette. They weren't very good fish and chips, but they tasted heavenly anyway. I called Zoulfia to say I would arrive late, and please could she pick up a bottle of wine because I'd need it. Then I went to the men's toilet to hold my sopping gloves under the blow dryer for half an hour.

We docked on time and I went below wondering if the bike would start, but less worried now; surely the worst they could do would be to wheel me off onto home turf? Again it fired up first time, and again I sent silent thanks to the guy who had fixed it.

Coming off the ferry, there was a light drizzle, but it soon cleared and I headed off onto the M20 and M25 until the turn-off for Surbiton and Wimbledon. Within two hours I was home, still damp, frozen, and aching all over, but overjoyed at the prospect of my own bed.

It took days for the aches and feeling of being cold inside to subside, even with a couple of visits to the local gym's steam room and sauna, but already I was plotting my return to France – only this time I would take the car and enjoy the comfort of heated seats, a GPS and music. No more winter biking for me; at least not marathons like that one.

Beudjeu called several times in my first week back and sent photos of himself, his son and his granddaughter to my mobile. 'When are you coming? You have to see your *kirvi, la petite* Monique, she's in Cognac now and has three children, we'll go and visit her.'

'Maybe next week,' I told him, 'or the week after that. I need to rest a bit and check the ferries.'

'You'll like it here. We're just by Le Dorat, you remember?'

'Sure I remember; how could I forget? Okay, I'll call you as soon as I've got a ticket for the boat.'

'Your Manouche family misses you!'

'And I miss my Manouche family,' I told him, and I meant it. Marseille might have been grim, but now I was excited again.

Le Dorat, of course. It was our old stomping ground and main stopping place all those years ago, when Zozo still had his horse-drawn caravan and Papi slept under the stars and Ghuno sang to them, and I felt my pulse quicken at the thought of going back there.

Jean-Pierre also called out of the blue, and I told him about my bike trip and how I was planning to go back the next week, this time to Le Dorat.

He laughed. 'You sure you don't want to fly to Bordeaux? You can borrow my motorbike; it's a T100 too. It's not so far to Limoges.'

'No more biking, at least not until the weather gets better!'

'Then we can meet anyway; I have to be in Bordeaux next week and then go back to Paris. Le Dorat is just north of Limoges and that's on the way for me.'

I said I'd call him when I was in France. Everything seemed to be falling into place; it was like *Back to the Future* come real. I still had time to make the trip before Brexit (or no Brexit) and booked a ferry to Dieppe this time, from Newhaven. It would save me a lot of miles on both sides of the channel, and oddly, even though the crossing time was more than twice that of the Dover to Calais route, the price was no more; if anything it was cheaper.

I called Beudjeu and gave him the news, and he sent me his address and said he'd come to fetch me when I got close. He also sent me another photo of himself. With his grey beard, paunch and owl-like glasses he looked nothing like the lean Beudjeu of old, even if he still had a full head of hair, but then I guess none of us looked like we used to.

Reunited

So it was that less than two weeks after I'd got back from Marseille I
rose before dawn on a Sunday and set off for Newhaven, just east
of Brighton, on empty roads. I checked in with time to spare but then
couldn't lock the car; every time I pushed the fob it just beeped and
refused to lock. But after about twenty minutes of confusion and
cursing keyless technology it suddenly dawned on me that I had a spare
set of keys in my suitcase inside the car, which meant the two keys were
cancelling each other out, one trying to lock the car, the other keeping
it open. What was wrong with the old simple keys?

The ferry left on time, and again I watched the white cliffs of southern England fade across the grey seas and tried to snooze. The weather
was fair and we docked to bright blue skies, and I wondered if maybe I
should have stuck with the motorbike after all; maybe I'd just got the
two journeys the wrong way around? But a vicious hailstorm just south
of Évreux banished that thought as pebble-sized bits of ice bounced off
the windscreen and visibility dropped to near zero. I was glad not to be
out in that, and instead just sat back and turned up the heating and the
volume on Howard Goodall's CD *Enchanted Voices*, one of my favourite
motorway music accompaniments, uplifting and soothing at the same
time.

It was getting dark already when I spotted the twin towers of
Chartres cathedral in the distance, and then, as I followed the N194
through the city centre, the light of another of the ubiquitous Ibis
hotels beckoned me in a picturesque square just under the cathedral. It
seemed like fate, so I pulled over and checked in, and called Beudjeu to
say I'd see him the next day. It seemed a smarter idea than ploughing
on through the darkness and arriving at his place at ten or eleven at
night.

'You're right,' he said. 'Call me when you get to Belloc and I'll come and fetch you; you'll never find our place alone.'

That was probably true. I'd already punched his address into the GPS, but nothing had shown up.

I also called Jean-Pierre and we agreed to meet for dinner on the Wednesday evening in Belloc, which is about thirty or forty miles north of Limoges. Finally I called Zoulfia, who told me that on her way to yoga she'd been evacuated from Ealing Broadway tube station by gun-toting black-clad police who'd then stormed inside.

'What was it?' I asked.

'No idea, I just got as far away as possible, but so many people just stayed right by the station filming on their mobiles. What if it was a bomb? People are stupid.'

'They are,' I agreed, and went in search of a steak frites and bottle of wine to put me to sleep.

Brilliant sunshine greeted me in the morning, and after a sumptuous breakfast of egg, salami, cheese, fruits, baguette and a couple of double espressos I set off on the final leg. I took the motorway and was soon eating up the miles, but the tyre pressure gauge warning kept flashing up on my dashboard. I stopped to check my tyres and asked the garage attendant how much I needed to put in the machine.

His eyebrows shot up and he looked at me in surprise. 'But air is free, monsieur!'

'Not in England it's not,' I told him. Maybe the French just didn't put up with as much bullshit as the English, or maybe the cost of the air was covered by their exorbitant fuel prices, around ten percent more than in England, which was the thing that had originally kicked off the nationwide yellow jacket protests in France.

Soon I passed out of the dreary flat landscape of northern France with its hundreds of electricity-generating windmills and was in the rolling hills of Limousin, which reminded me of the South Downs in England. Shortly after midday I pulled into the main square of Belloc, where Beudjeu was waiting with his 'new' wife Zaza, Pesi having apparently left him some twenty years before. We jumped out of our cars and embraced and kissed each other on the cheeks, four times according to the local custom, then just stood holding each other's arms, looking and shaking our heads. He had filled out and wore glasses now, but otherwise he was exactly the same, all his mannerisms, his way of talking.

'You're here, you came to find us, I can't believe it,' he said.

'Me neither, and it wasn't easy to find you. Marseille wasn't good, but it's good to see you again. I've missed you.'

I followed him about ten miles down tiny roads until we pulled into their smallholding. There were no other houses around, just their small one-room home with a bathroom and outside toilet, all of which they'd built themselves, and several caravans which visiting family members used in the summer.

'We have to go and see Blon and Niglo,' Beudjeu said once I'd unpacked my things into one of the caravans. 'They're not far, just by Le Dorat.'

Before we left he gave me a knife with a bone handle engraved with a motif of a hedgehog and horse-dawn *varda*. 'So you can eat,' he said with a smile. Some things hadn't changed after all, and it's a present I'll treasure.

We drove off but after just a few miles stopped when Beudjeu saw Niglo's car outside a house. A large group of Manouche were there cooking over a huge fire; there were Niglo and Blon, along with Nanoon, Ringo and Jean-Luis, who had been children the last time I had been with them, but they remembered me, and again we embraced and laughed and the years disappeared.

Everyone was a bit older, but everyone was the same too, Blon with his permanent half-smile, Niglo with his cheeky grin, exactly how I remembered them. Both were still lean and wiry, unlike Beudjeu, Blon in black jeans and black leather jacket, fair-haired Niglo in blue jeans and a black leather jacket of his own, with a flat cap to hide his balding pate. Blon was fifty-eight years old, four years younger than Beudjeu, and Niglo just fifty-six. Sadly their younger brother Pepite was missing, having passed away with cancer at the tender age of twenty-two. So many had been taken by cancer, not just Pepite but Narte, Dalila, young Volka and Nina as well, while Chiclo drank himself to death and both Matzos, Pantoon's father and Volka's husband, had been killed in car crashes. I wondered if the high incidence of cancer was because of heavy smoking or a diet of too much char-burned meat. Or both.

Blon came over and thrust some bread and a hunk of meat at me. '*Niglo*,' he said, meaning 'hedgehog', not his brother Niglo. 'We caught a couple today; this is the last piece. Do you still like it?'

I took a bite; it was delicious and memories flooded back, but at the same time I was a bit uneasy about eating hedgehog now. 'It's a protected species in England; there's not so many any more,' I said.

'Same here,' he told me. 'We don't eat them so much now and we never take the pregnant ones, but still it's good sometimes.' He shrugged and smiled. Then he reminded me of the time he and Beudjeu rescued me from the *klistey* in Marseille. 'You remember that?' he asked, stuffing his own piece of baguette with a spicy Merguez sausage.

'Sure I do,' I answered, laughing, and again the years dropped away. They remembered everything of our old times together and we ate and ate and reminisced. There was enough on the barbecue for fifty people, ribs, sausages and chicken, but we were less than a dozen even when some of the women turned up.

They tested me on my Manouche.

'Say "wine".' Niglo grinned at me.

'*Mol*,' I said.

'Look!'

'*Dik!*'

'Drink.'

'*Pi.*'

'Hand.'

'*Maast.*'

'Bravo! You are still Manouche.' Blon clapped me on the back.

'How about "Koki's hand"?' Niglo said mischievously, and everyone burst out laughing. Koki, on his first day's work ever at a sawmill, lost the first three fingers of his right hand, but he still played the guitar better than most, strumming with his thumb and little finger while his left hand moved dexterously over the frets.

'And now he does the housework too,' Beudjeu said. 'Tac-Tac left him in Marseille to come here, she was fed up with him beating her, but he followed her and he's a different person. He's not angry like before, he's very quiet, and she smokes and drinks in front of him, which she'd never dare to do before.'

I took out a book about British Gypsies with a glossary of Romany words and we compared them. Some were almost exactly the same, such as *mas* for 'meat' or *dik* for 'look' or *chore* for 'steal', even if in Manouche *chor* without the long 'e' is a moustache and *chorlo* is 'poor'. Other words were completely different; for example, the Manouche *maast* for 'hand' became *fam* in British Romany, while *niglo* for 'hedge-hog' in Manouche became *hotchi*. Even so, I was convinced that there were enough similarities that a French Manouche and British Romany would be able to quite easily hold a conversation if they ever met.

We stayed for a couple of hours, sawing off pieces of meat with our knives, moving the fire inside a barn when fat drops of rain started falling, and talking of the past.

'There's a lot of English living around here,' Beudjeu told me. 'Whenever I meet one I ask if he knows *Nadjo*, but none of them do.'

'Well, there are 60 million people in Britain, and it's a common enough name,' I said, amused.

We agreed to meet Blon and Niglo the next morning and drive to see my *kirvi*, Monique, who was living about thirty miles away, just across the border with the region of Charente.

There was an empty caravan next to Beudjeu's house which had been made ready for me. Zaza had put an electric heater on and clean sheets on the bed; it was warm and snug, and I listened to the patter of rain on the roof and the cries of foxes and hoots of owls and felt completely at peace with the world before falling into a deep sleep full of lurid dreams. I stayed unconscious until the roosters began their dawn chorus.

(L-R) Niglo, Beudjeu and Blon outside their house near Le Dorat, 2019.

Ghuno and Monique

We waited in vain for Blon and Niglo before setting off late in the morning, just me, Beudjeu and Zaza.

'Probably they drank too much and are still asleep,' Beudjeu remarked, but I knew from past experience that prearranged meetings are a loose arrangement at best amongst the Manouche; if anything more pressing comes up they see no reason to keep to any kind of schedule. Neither Blon nor Niglo had telephones; their wives did, but they had gone to work, cleaners in local houses and restaurants.

As we drove I mentioned my suspicions about Lele in Marseille and how he'd suddenly 'found' my laptop and camera.

'You're probably right,' Beudjeu said. 'Lele is always up to no good. He probably didn't realise who you were, but almost certainly it was him all along; he just saw you as a *gadjo* and an opportunity. There's no respect from the young any more. It's why we left Marseille; it's a bad place. There's nothing for us there.'

For the most part you notice far more on a motorbike than in a car, but one thing I hadn't seen on the trip to Marseille was any speed cameras, despite the numerous warning signs. Beudjeu pointed them out from the car; every single one was burnt to a crisp or wrapped in thick black tape by the yellow jacket protestors. Four months in and their protests against the cost of living were still going strong; they occupied most of the roundabouts, often blocking traffic unless you showed your support. At one roundabout neither Beudjeu nor Zaza were sure which way to go, and we circled five times, watched in consternation by the protestors who probably wondered what this weird Englishman was doing, until Beudjeu waved my yellow jacket and we finally exited to rousing cheers.

Monique was waiting for us with her husband Mamay, who was also from Mirabeau, at their small house surrounded by fields at the end of a tiny track in the middle of nowhere. We embraced and exchanged kisses. She had become plump like her mother Pesi and already had three children of her own, two of them married, but she was all smiles.

'I've been looking for you on the internet,' she told me.

'But you don't know how to spell my name!' I said, and she giggled and told me how she remembered our boat holiday in the Camargue.

Beudjeu and Mamay sat and smoked at the table (Mamay made roll-ups, but Beudjeu had taken up vaping), while I read my book on British Gypsies and Monique and Zaza started to prepare couscous. The Manouche seem to be able to sit and talk endlessly about nothing much at all, but after an hour or two I asked if we could go and visit Ghuno while we waited for the food. Apparently she was only about five miles away.

'But Paquili isn't there, he's gone to hospital,' Beudjeu said.

'I don't care about that,' I told him. 'I want to see Ghuno. Remember, she was the first Manouche to speak to me, so she's special.'

'What, you want to take her back to England?' Mamay said, laughing.

We went anyway and found them living with two other families on a small patch of land by a potholed lane surrounded by woods. They were all in caravans, without running water or toilets. They were living as they always had.

Paquili was still there – he hadn't made it to the hospital yet – but I hardly recognised him. The one-time strongman was a shell of his former self, shrunken, with wispy strands of white hair and a grey beard. We embraced and he told me he'd just had open heart surgery a couple of months earlier; he wasn't well.

Then Ghuno stepped out of her caravan and ambled over and we gave each other a huge hug.

'I knew you would come back,' she said. 'At the end of last year I saw a white butterfly, and I thought about you.'

Which was just insane, because that was about the time I had first mooted the idea of finding my Manouche family again.

'What's this with white butterflies?' Beudjeu asked.

'They bring good news,' Ghuno answered him. 'If a white butterfly comes to you, then you can be sure it's bringing good news.'

'I remember,' I told her. I still couldn't believe we were having this conversation.

Ghuno was dressed in a floral skirt with a blue cardigan and a chunky white scarf, with a belt of dozens of clothes pegs around her waist. She was wearing glasses now and her hair was grey but still thick; her dark eyes twinkled as ever, looking over-large through her lenses. She'd filled out; she was still tiny but now resembled more a well-fed robin redbreast than a starving sparrow, and she was in rude good health.

'I still work all day, washing, cleaning, and I drink a litre of wine a day,' she told me, and she invited us into her caravan. She was seventy-one years old now, a bit less than I'd thought but still a good age, and her mind was still as sharp as a razor.

The caravan was warmed by a gas stove and as clean as ever, despite one door blackened by a fire after Paquili left his trousers to dry above the stove. Ghuno and I drank wine, the others coffee.

'What about Bianca?' I asked.

'Oh, she's fifty years old now, she's not too far away. She has her own children, you know.'

'And La Muette?'

'Passed away.'

'So you just live here now? You don't travel any more?'

'I go to Lourdes every year, but not to Les Saintes; that's finished. But I like Lourdes.'

'So you're Catholic now?'

'Not really.' Ghuno smiled and refilled our glasses. 'I just like it there; it's peaceful.'

I asked who the land they were living on belonged to.

'It's mine,' Ghuno said. 'But they're going to build a new road here, so we'll have to leave. They'll have to give me another piece of land.'

She didn't know where that might be, and I wondered where on earth this new road would be going from or to; there were enough roads around connecting all the main towns in the area.

As we chatted on, Paquili kept a hand cocked to his ear, trying to follow the conversation. He looked lost.

'I wasn't going to come because you said you wouldn't be here.' Beudjeu gave him a dig in the ribs. 'But Nadjo said he wanted to see Ghuno even without you!'

Paquili just grunted in response. He was still rarely allowed into Ghuno's caravan and still slept in his van. He cut a sad figure.

After an hour or so we took our leave, and after final embraces Ghuno simply wandered off to her washing lines behind the caravan without a backwards glance, even before we'd got into the car, just as she had forty years earlier when we'd first met. I wondered if I'd ever see her again.

'They have money, you know,' Beudjeu said as we left. 'I don't know why they still live like that.'

Back at Mamay's house we sat at the table and sliced salami and bread with our knives while the women finished preparing the couscous. When it was finally served we had to resort to spoons for the first time since I'd arrived, and the men ate at the table while the women stood with their plates in a corner of the room.

Before we left, Mamay put on a song by a Gypsy guitarist which viciously attacked President Macron. 'Racist' and 'cretin' were some of the kinder words used to describe the president.

'The Manouche all support the yellow vests,' Mamay said. 'The president only cares about rich people, not about us.'

Astonishingly, it seemed the Manouche were also becoming politicised. Apparently there was even a Manouche mayor somewhere in Languedoc.

The author with his God daughter Monique, Charente 2019.

And with Ghuno and Paquili at their campsite, Charente 2019.

Le Dorat

The next day we went to visit Blon and Niglo at their house outside Le Dorat. On the way Beudjeu showed me the spot where Chocote had died after his car left the road and crashed into a tree ten years earlier, then we stopped at Le Dorat's graveyard to pay our respects to Chocote and Oumlo. They were buried together in their own mausoleum, which was decorated with all manner of statues of saints and family photographs, with pride of place at the front given to a small stone statue of a hedgehog.

'My mother never really recovered from Pepite dying so young,' Beudjeu told me. 'And when she passed away, Chocote felt abandoned; he was always sad.'

Pantoon's father, Matzo, was buried in another mausoleum nearby, and Beudjeu had paid € 5,000 for his own mausoleum, which was alongside.

'It makes it easier for everyone when I go,' Beudjeu said.

'I think I'll let myself be cremated,' I told him. 'What I'd really like is to be put in a boat and set on fire like the old Vikings.'

'Some of us go to the fire, but mostly we prefer to be buried,' he said.

We also visited our old stopping place in Le Dorat. It was still there, but now the entrance was blocked by a chain and a sign forbidding travellers to stay.

We arrived at Blon and Niglo's place shortly before midday and found them and several other *rom* standing around a deep hole which they had dug to expose their sewerage pipes. The pipes had sunk and the waste wasn't flowing properly any more.

'Oh, Nadjo.' Blon came over and offered his wrist to shake; his hands weren't really in a shakeable state. 'We need to raise the pipes, put new

ones in. But enough for today; let's have a beer and then some food.'
He went to wash his hands while the rest of us popped beers.

Twenty years earlier Chocote, ever the visionary, had led his
company out of the despair of Marseille back to Le Dorat, where for
just € 3,000 he'd purchased a run-down farmhouse and about a hectare
of land. Oumlo had passed away peacefully after a short illness two
years later, but together the company had cleared the land and reno-
vated the farmhouse, which was now divided into two halves, one half
for Blon and his family, the other for Niglo and his wife and children.
There was also a new extension which housed one of Niglo's sons and
his wife, and three caravans on the site with the families of other relatives. In all there were about thirty people living on the site, including
children.

Although Chocote himself had died ten years earlier in that car accident, his legacy was this beautiful place surrounded by lush countryside.
It was about as perfect a place as I could imagine for an extended
Manouche family to live together and preserve their way of life, such a
far cry from the slums and depredations of Marseille. Everything was
clean and well looked after, the children were impeccably behaved and
showed respect to their elders, and the common language was
Manouche again. Even if the big flat-screen televisions were on in both
houses, no one was looking at them. One thing I noticed, though, was
that, just as in Beudjeu's house, there was nothing on the walls apart from
the televisions and a few photographs. Gone were all the old knickknacks
of copper work, china and shotguns; it all seemed a bit spartan.

'We're well here,' Blon told me. 'We have showers and toilets and hot
water; it's much better than when we had to wash in a bowl.'

'I remember when you said it was healthier to shit outside,' I said.

Blon laughed; a grin was never far away from his face. 'Ah, yes, I
remember that too.' He squatted down and stuck his backside out.
'Like this, down in the docks,' He chuckled again. 'No, we are much
better off now.'

Some of them worked; Blon himself had done five years as a
dustman before back pain made him stop. Others worked on local

farms or in construction, or as waiters in restaurants. The teenagers were noticeably taller than the older Manouche and were all schooled.

'We're the last ones who never went to school, and we're the last ones who travelled,' Blon said. 'I still can't read or write, but I think it's a good thing that our children can. They have a better future.'

Blon lit a fire for the inevitable barbecue, and we used our knives to carve off hunks of meat and stuff them into slices of baguette with salad. Again the men sat together and the women kept to themselves, including the young. That tradition had remained, although when I pointed it out Niglo laughed and darted across the courtyard to squeeze between the women.

'Is that better?' he asked, before returning to his place with the men.

Blon produced a 2003 bottle of fine Bordeaux wine to wash down our rough fare.

'A good time for a celebration,' he said, splashing the wine into my plastic cup. 'It's good to have you back. Come again in the summer; we'll go to the river for a picnic. Don't forget us.'

'I won't, you can be sure.' I was feeling emotional again.

We left shortly after lunch because I'd agreed to meet Jean-Pierre in the evening. Beudjeu wouldn't let me drive after drinking and dropped me off in Belloc, where Jean-Pierre was waiting.

'I remember you,' Beudjeu said to him. 'Maybe we can come back again for the *vendange*?'

They both laughed, and Beudjeu told me to call him when we'd finished our dinner and he would collect me. I was still full from the barbecue but ate a plate of scallops while Jean-Pierre tucked into pig's cheek. We remembered the old days, probably our best days, we both agreed.

'I want to retire within a year, go back to Tête Rouge and live there,' Jean-Pierre said. 'You must come to visit.'

I will, of course; it's inevitable. Oddly I'm ambivalent about France, but I know I'm tied to the Manouche and Jean-Pierre will always be one of my best friends. And Tête Rouge is only a couple of hours away from Limoges.

When we finished Beudjeu duly turned up to take me back to my caravan, where again I slept the sleep of the dead.

Another night, as we were driving home in the dusk, Beudjeu suddenly pulled over when he saw a large gathering of vans and assorted cars parked up outside a barn.

'Manouche,' he said. 'Let's see what's happening.'

There were maybe two dozen men grouped outside the barn, drinking beers and smoking. They looked at me curiously and nodded at Beudjeu, and they spoke rapidly together in Manouche.

'You want to see?' Beudjeu asked me as the men started filing into the barn.

'What is it?'

'A cockfight.'

I shrugged. I was both curious and repelled. 'Okay, but isn't that illegal?'

'Yes, but it happens. I don't really like it either and I never bet, but it happens, it's very popular.'

Inside it was gloomy and crowded; there were fifty or more men inside, no women, and most seemed to be French. There was a lot of shouting and large amounts of money were changing hands until the MC held up his hands and an expectant hush descended. He was a big, thickset Frenchman with a flat cap and a luxurious beard decorated with pieces of silver kitchen foil twisted into it.

Two men advanced into the circle, each holding a cock, one black and white, the other jet black, and both with wicked blades attached to their legs. The MC took a large swig of whisky – single malt, I noticed – and blew a spray of alcohol over the heads of the two cocks, who were then released.

It was savage, bloody and quick. In less than a minute the black cock lay under the claws of his opponent, blood gushing from his neck. I felt both sick and full of adrenaline.

'We should go,' I said to Beudjeu as the owner of the winning cock picked the bird up and carefully put it in a cage.

The owner caught my eye and grinned. 'You are English, then?'

174

I said I was.

'This is an English fighting cock, the best!' And he laughed, pocketing a handful of banknotes.

'And the other?'

'Spanish. They are good too, but I like the English birds most.'

Beudjeu and I congratulated the man and quietly took our leave.

'It's wrong,' I said. 'I didn't really like it.'

'Yes, it's wrong, but lots of things are, and like I said, it happens. You can't change that.'

*

I stayed for a week before retracing my way to Dieppe and Newhaven.

'I feel you like a brother,' Beudjeu told me as I got ready to leave. 'You will come back, won't you?'

'I feel the same, and you can be sure I'll be back.' And I would be.

I left happy in the knowledge not only that had I found my old friends and Manouche family again, and that this time we definitely wouldn't lose contact now that we all had mobile phones, but also that they were well, as close-knit as ever, living in such beautiful surroundings and with their culture more or less intact. They are now living within society rather than ostracised and at the bottom of the pile, but still outside it, a kind of parallel existence. They no longer have to travel from nowhere to nowhere; they have found their place, somewhere to belong, and in a way I am envious. I live in a country I no longer recognise, my children are spread across the world, I still struggle to identify with anywhere and still feel rootless. In that sense I suspect my Manouche family are richer than many of us.

Chocote's and Oumlo's grave, Le Dorat 2019.

Glossary

Gypsies are generally accepted as having originated in India, migrating by different routes around 1,000 years ago, some up through Afghanistan and eventually into Eastern Europe, others taking a southern route along both sides of the Mediterranean before entering Spain and France. The word 'Gypsy' is based on 'Gypo' or 'Egyptian', which many presumed them to be when they first arrived in Europe, but their language, although not written, has definite Sanskrit roots. Everywhere they have settled, their language has adopted from and adapted to the locality, which is why there are significant differences between French Manouche and British Romanies or the Jenische from Germany. Clearly many of the words my company used had German origins, I guess from the Sinti influence. But there are many striking similarities between the Gypsy languages used in each country too, and as I've noted I'm sure they could conduct a basic conversation between themselves. Below is a glossary of what I will call Manouche, but the spelling is phonetic and the interpretation is my own.

Ab	To come	*Chai*	Girl/daughter
Abistundayi?	What time is it?	*Chavo*	Boy/son
Affo	Monkey	*Chero*	Head
Ahso	Rabbit	*Chi*	It's nothing
Akhun	Each	*Chiben*	Bed
Al	He is	*Chiclo*	Little bird
Alt	Always	*Chigilo*	Dirty
Altra	To wait	*Chila*	Cold
Alray	To stop	*Chip*	Tongue
Altz	Often	*Choca*	Beautiful
Apbeshtu	To sit down	*Chor*	Moustache
Apiarte	To hunt	*Chore*	To steal
Archt	Difficult	*Chorlo*	Poor
Arjha tu?	How are you?	*Chucel*	Dog
Arno	Cockerel	*Chum*	Kiss
Auto	Car	*Chuvel*	Woman
Bachiramen	To go for a walk	*Corba*	Bucket/basket
Bal	Hair	*Cordives*	Day/today
Balo	Pig	*Cort*	Short
Baro	Big	*Dayarchte*	To be careful
Baroles	To make love	*Dayla*	Rain
Baysa	Brush	*Delal*	Below
Beng	The devil	*Delli*	Bad
Bengelo	Magic	*Dengo*	To think
Berghi	Mountain	*Dent* (plural *denti*)	Tooth
Blume	Flower	*Devel*	God
Bok	Hunger	*Dik*	Look
Bravelo	Rich	*Dika*	To look at
Broll	Pear	*Dinelo*	Stupid
Buldagh	More	*Divesparli*	Yesterday
Cam	Sun	*Djaferra*	To travel
Campana	Watch (timepiece)	*Djajina*	To know
Can	Small	*Djangamen*	To wake up
Candelli	To smell bad	*Djaouna*	To listen
Capa	Hat	*Djatova*	To wash
Caramaskri	Pistol	*Djatrapotut/ Djatrapa*	To catch
Catzo	Glass	*Djochino*	To cut
Chachirik	Correct	*Djogino*	To buy
Chacho	You're right	*Djino*	I know

Djipen	Life	*Hep*	Hole
Draka	Grapes	*Hoyamen*	Angry
Drin	Inside/into	*Hroy*	Spoon
Durgh	Far	*Ilab*	Dead
Elylercht	Empty	*Ilopilo*	To be drunk
Escaney	Early/now	*Imishto*	Comfortable/it's
Eschana	When		good
Faltelman	I like it	*Itsa*	Hot
Faynti	Enemy	*Ja*	To go
Faysana	Pheasant	*Jedika*	To take a look
Fehta	Party	*Jaghamengey*	To go and
Flasche	Bottle		eat/let's eat
Floymi	Plum	*Jai-yva*	To understand
Fraidigoh	Happy	*Jala*	Okay/I agree
Fuchsa	Fox	*Jamengey*	Let's go
Ga	Not	*Japadramen*	To go swimming
Gabla	Fork	*Ja-ouna*	To listen/I'm
Gachacho	To be		listening
	mistaken/you're	*Jasorva*	To go to sleep
	wrong	*Jatuke!*	Go away!/be off!
Gadje	Non-Gypsy	*Jet*	Oil
	(female)	*Jose*	Trousers
Gadjo	Non-Gypsy (male)	*Kaghni*	Chicken
Gaiga	Violin	*Kai?*	Where?
Galcho	Bad	*Kaki*	Like this/like that
Garcht	Easy	*Kalou*	Black
Gatayach	Cheap	*Kamlo*	Kind
Gerelgalarme	Quiet/not noisy	*Kan*	Ears
Gha	To eat	*Kangli*	Comb
Ghaben	Food	*Kascht*	Wood
Gharnit	Never	*Kate*	Here
Ghati	Blood	*Kelap*	To dance
Ghrima	Belt	*Keme?*	Do you want?
Ghrovova	To cry	*Kemo*	I want
Giely	Song	*Kergh*	House
Godjebro	Clever	*Keta*	Chain/necklace
Grai	Horse	*Kibla*	Basin
Guitarra	Guitar	*Kichi-bergsch-tut?*	How old are you?
Gustri	Ring	*Kichivolel?*	How much?

Kino	Tired	*Mero*	Sea
Kiral	Cheese	*Mishto*	Good
Kirgha	Shoes	*Mol*	Wine
Kiriasi	Cherry	*Mooka*	A fly
Kirvi	Godmother	*Morghpal*	Brother
Kirvo	Godfather	*Morgphen*	Sister
Kishta	Box/coffin	*Mossit*	Air
Klistey	Police	*Moy*	Face
Kni	Knee	*Mukotgoless*	To lend
Kora	Walnut	*Mulesdrikishta*	Coffin
Kosh	To swear/promise	*Mulo*	Death/death
Kuramen	To fight		spirit
Kwa	Penis	*Murga*	Cat
Lachidagh	Best	*Mutra*	Mother
Lachirat	Goodnight	*Nac*	Nose
Lacho	Good	*Nacht*	Night
Lachodevis	Good day/hello	*Nasha*	To run
Leidigoh	Sad/unhappy	*Nasilo*	Illness
Larme	Noise	*Nayo*	Fingernail
Leer	Empty	*Neri*	Black (*kalou* is
Lefte	Lips		more common)
Lohn	Salt	*Nevo*	New
Lokass	Slow/slowly	*Nisl*	Summer
Lolo	Red	*Niglo* (plural *nigli*)	Hedgehog
Lorvey	Money	*Norgh*	Close
Lungo	Long	*Nuvesch*	Forest
Lotutbal	To follow	*Ockso*	Bull
Lumpi	The washing	*Om*	I am
Macho	Fish	*Oranga*	Orange
Mal	Friend	*Ordaygo?*	What are you
Manbok	I'm hungry		looking at?
Mantrouche	I'm thirsty	*Orva*	Yes
Marga	Thin	*Oske?*	Why?
Maro	Bread	*Oura*	Watch
Maroltut	To kill	*Pado*	Full
Mas	Meat	*Pagado*	Broken
Mato	Drunk	*Pago*	To break
Me	Me	*Pakromen*	Thank you
Mer	Us	*Palay*	Afterwards

Pani	Water	*Sa*	To laugh
Pash	Less	*Schadt!*	What a pity!
Pashleste	His home/house	*Schanki*	Woodwork
Pashmende	My home/house	*Schdadi*	Hat
Patria	Leaves	*Schera*	Scissors
Pefro	Pepper	*Schik*	Earth/ground
Pesi	Fat/heavy	*Schlercht*	Danger
Petlada	Bunk	*Schpeko*	Ham
Phulo	Lazy	*Schport*	Late
Pi!	Drink!	*Schurin*	Knife
Piap	To drink	*Schut*	Vinegar
Piramen	To embrace	*Schwach*	Weak
Piray	Love	*Schwekimutra*	Mother-in-law
Piraytut	I love you	*Schwekivetro*	Father-in-law
Pisla	Small/a little	*Shouna*	To hear
Plato	Plate	*Shouno*	I hear
Pral	Above	*Sik*	Quickly
Praltaysa	The next day	*Sikla*	To teach
Pudigha	Never	*Soukai*	Gold
Puent	Nail	*Sorva*	To sleep
Puro	Old	*Spengli*	Clothes peg
Pushka	Gun	*Spieli*	Game
Pushtabo	Pen	*Spielimengen*	To go and enjoy
Pustolo	Chair/seat		oneself
Queschki	Prune	*Spori*	Animal
Rada (plural *radi*)	Wheel		spoor/trail
Raka	To speak	*Stanga*	Branch
Rakli	Non-Gypsy	*Still*	Calm/tranquil
	(female, *gadje* is	*Strempi*	Socks
	more common)	*Tatta*	Daddy
Raklo	Non-Gypsy (male,	*Tayach*	Expensive
	gadjo is more	*Taysa*	Tomorrow
	common)	*Telari*	Plate
Rara	Always	*Tief*	Deep
Reria	Leg	*Tikeno*	Small
Rocka	Jacket	*Tikinichai*	Baby girl
Rom	Man	*Tikinichavo*	Baby boy
Romni	Woman/wife	*Tila*	Plank
Rotso	Snot	*Tisha*	Table

181

Trasho	Fear/to be afraid	*Yek*	One
Trouche	Thirst	*Dui*	Two
Tschacho	Truth	*Trin*	Three
Tschapo	Vagina	*Stach*	Four
Tu	You	*Pansch*	Five
Tuai	You are	*Schop*	Six
Tubili	Cigarette	*Efta*	Seven
Tut	Milk	*Octo*	Eight
Tutshia	Breast	*Ena*	Nine
Ubudo	Cousin	*Desh*	Ten
Vaco	Sheep	*Deshyek*	Eleven
Vago	Car	*Deshdui*	Twelve
Varahpen	Journey	*Deshtrin*	Thirteen
Varda	Caravan	*Deshstach*	Fourteen
Varo	To drive	*Deshpansch*	Fifteen
Vartigo	To finish	*Deshschop*	Sixteen
Vatro	Father	*Deshefta*	Seventeen
Velto	World	*Deshocto*	Eighteen
Vent	Winter	*Deshena*	Nineteen
Vesch	A wood/copse	*Bish*	Twenty
Vey	To come	*Bishyek*	Twenty-one
Weiss	White	*Trianda*	Thirty
Yacca	Eye	*Duibish*	Forty
Yak	Fire	*Pahsel*	Fifty
Yepla	Apple	*Trinbish*	Sixty
Yeschto	Next	*Trinbishdesh*	Seventy
Ygaremligo	Different	*Stachbish*	Eighty
Yop –	Him/her	*Stachbishdesh*	Ninety
Zerverik	Left	*Schel*	One hundred
Zinder	Poor thing!	*Duischel*	Two hundred
	(expression of	*Toysto*	One thousand
	sympathy)		
Zoibagh	Clean		
Zolles	Strong		

Acknowledgements

I would like to thank everyone at the Choir Press and especially the editor, Harriet Evans, for all their support and hard work which made the process of publication so painless. I'd also like to thank Alice Jolly, John-Paul Flintoff and everyone at the Arvon Centre for their mentoring sessions, which taught me again how to find pleasure in writing.

Milton Keynes UK
Ingram Content Group UK Ltd.
UKHW020229301123
433483UK00016B/1041